ISBN 0-9727783-0-6

Written By Richard Labus & Minimol Rajan
Editing & Layout by Nancy Gall
Front Cover Artwork by Grant Seeker Pro Inc
Software Program Development by Guild Soft Pvt. Ltd.

Special thanks to:
Suzanne Denham
Diana Webster
Small Business Administration

Simulation developed from materials provided by Westinghouse Corporation
under contract to the Department of Energy.

Some images used herein were obtained from IMSI's Master Photos
Collection, San Rafael, CA.

Contents

Contents

Welcome

Thank you for choosing Grant Seeker Pro™! At Grant Seeker Pro we have done our absolute best to ensure that you succeed in your grant seeking ventures.

Grant Seeker Pro™ will guide you in your research of over $1.5 trillion dollars in Federal funding. This funding is made available to virtually every business entity, private foundation, and private individual across the United States, Puerto Rico, the US Virgin Islands, Guam and every other US held territory or possession. Until now access to this funding has been extremely difficult to locate because of the sheer size of the government database. Grant Seeker Pro™ has taken down this barrier in it's quest for the ultimate grant research tool. With the typing of a single word you will be able to search the entire federal database in mere seconds. Best of all there is no Internet connection required. This is an entirely self-contained product that was designed to operate on almost any PC.

In order to begin, it is strongly suggested that you read this guide cover to cover. While grant seeking can present challenges, in almost all cases the rewards at the end make the whole process worthwhile. Whether you are seeking money for your business or your non-profit charity, whether it is education or medical assistance, Grant Seeker Pro™ can help you achieve your goals.

Contrary to popular belief, grant seeking is not as difficult as it appears on the surface. If you are generally well organized you will have little trouble completing the process. Seventy five percent of grant seeking is research. That is where your Grant Seeker Pro™ software comes in. This program was specifically designed to not only aid the professional grant writer but also the everyday person seeking funding for their business, church, education or virtually any other need they may have. You will have the ability to search the entire grants database in a matter of seconds. Once you find the perfect grant you will be able to create your application letter and the federally required application with just a few key strokes. While you are awaiting the response you will be able to use the Business Plan Wizard to create a professional budget or business plan that will impress any bank or grant-giving institution.

Let's Get it Together

Behind every giant retailer, mass merchandiser, or one person play there is an idea. The passion that drives those ideas has made this the greatest country on earth!

Obviously you have the idea and the passion or you would not be reading this. Passion for the idea will drive you through this entire process. You must be prepared to be tested mentally on more than one occasion. You must be ready to have your idea questioned, criticized and sometimes even ridiculed.

As you search through the Grant Seeker Pro™ CD keep in mind that times they are a changing and that there is a time for every good idea. It will be your passion that makes the funder see that the time has come to bring your idea to fruition.

As you begin, you need to gather all the personal information available about you that will convince the funding agency that you are the right person for this job. This is not unlike preparing a resume. You will want to review every piece of information that even remotely applies to your idea. Have you previously managed business programs before? Have you operated a store? Have you managed the family budget? All of this can be used to help persuade the funding agency that you have the necessary abilities.

Learn to capitalize on inexperience... turn a perceived disadvantage into an advantage.

Learn to capitalize on inexperience. If there is an aspect of the program that you cannot manage, talk about the people you plan to hire to handle that task. Turn a perceived disadvantage into an advantage.

> *During the 1984 presidential election campaign Ronald Reagan was asked to answer questions concerning his age. The press was questioning his abilities because he was 78 years old. His response was, "Far be it from me to take advantage of my opponent's youth and inexperience" He was able to quickly turn a perceived disadvantage into an advantage.*

Do not let a lack of experience in certain areas slow you down either. If you feel that you have a weakness that may affect the outcome of your proposal, then be sure to address in your proposal how you will overcome that weakness. A funder that is giving away money has a responsibility to ensure that it is used properly.

When you apply to an organization, keep in mind that you will need to align yourself as closely as possible to the funding agencies goals. Do not radically alter your idea just so that you can apply to a different agency, otherwise you risk losing the core that drives your passion. Simply be open to modification. Keeping the objective in front of you at all times will aid you in staying on track and on task throughout the whole process. If you are a teacher who wants to help clothe and feed some of your younger students, then draw a picture of how they will look in shiny new shoes with a smile on their faces from a full belly.

When talking to others within the field or even outside of the field about your project, keep in mind that they may not have the same passion for it that you do. For this reason the criticism may seem harsh. While one person may positively love your idea another may hate it. Keep a written record of the criticisms so that you can refer to them later. An idea or additional input from someone else may sound great at the time, but this is your baby so do not jump the gun and start making modifications. Take your time, analyze the suggestion, weigh the merits, then decide how to use the information gained.

Do you have everything together? You have the idea, you have the talent, you have the experience and you have the commitment. Well then let's move on.

General Introduction

We read nearly every day about government spending, but what most people don't realize and what you are about to find out is that many of us are eligible to receive some of the money the government gives away every year. There are thousands of grant programs for established businesses and newcomers. Whether it's to develop a unique invention, continue or change your career path through education, work at your artistic vocation or simply obtaining help with living expenses, there are numerous sources out there for you to tap into.

Generally, if you are an organized, detail-oriented person who can follow instructions, chances are you can qualify for a grant.

How to identify the programs you qualify for is the biggest stumbling block to those that think they might qualify for government funds in some way. The key to obtaining grant money is not a giant secret. Generally, if you are an organized, detail-oriented person who can follow instructions, chances are you can qualify for a grant. The following chapters will detail everything you need to know in order to write and apply for a grant.

Throughout the book numerous references are made to the Grant Seeker Pro™ CD. This CD will be the primary tool for locating your grant sources. While references may be made to other sources, we are quite certain that what can be found elsewhere can also be found on the Grant Seeker Pro™ CD.

Who Has the Money?

The Federal Government

The single largest donor to Non Profit Organizations (NPOs) and private business is the United States government. Funding is available for everything from adult literacy campaigns and legal assistance to business to photographic art at local museums.

Currently, programs are being classified by the Government Services Administration into fifteen types of assistance. Benefits and services of the programs are provided through seven financial types of assistance and eight non-financial types of assistance. The following list defines the types of assistance which are available through the programs.

Funding is available for everything from adult literacy campaigns to photographic art at local museums.

Financial Assistance

Formula Grants

(173 Programs) Allocations of money to states or their subdivisions in accordance with distribution formulas prescribed by law or administrative regulation for activities of a continuing nature not confined to a specific project.

Project Grants

(889 Programs) The funding, for fixed or known periods, of specific projects. Project grants can include fellowships, scholarships, research grants, training grants, traineeships, experimental and demonstration grants, evaluation grants, planning grants, technical assistance grants, survey grants, and construction grants.

Direct Payments for Specified Use

(138 Programs) Financial assistance from the federal government provided directly to individuals, private

The single largest donor to Non Profit Organizations (NPOs) is the United States Government.

firms, and other private institutions to encourage or subsidize a particular activity by conditioning the receipt of the assistance on a particular performance by the recipient. This does not include solicited contracts for the procurement of goods and services for the federal government.

Direct Payments with Unrestricted Use

(38 Programs) Financial assistance from the federal government provided directly to beneficiaries who satisfy federal eligibility requirements with no restrictions being imposed on the recipient as to how the money is spent. Included are payments under retirement, pension, and compensatory programs.

Direct Loans

(44 Programs) Financial assistance provided through the lending of Federal monies for a specific period of time, with a reasonable expectation of repayment. Such loans may or may not require the payment of interest.

Guaranteed/Insured Loans

(61 Programs) Programs in which the federal government makes an arrangement to indemnify a lender against part or all of any defaults by those responsible for repayment of loans.

Insurance

(12 Programs) Financial assistance provided to assure reimbursement for losses sustained under specified conditions. Coverage may be provided directly by the federal government or through private carriers and may or may not involve the payment of premiums.

Non-Financial Assistance

Sale, Exchange, or Donation of Property and Goods

(23 Programs) Programs which provide for the sale, exchange, or donation of federal real property, personal property, commodities, and other goods including land, buildings, equipment, food and drugs. This does not include the loan of, use of, or access to federal facilities or property.

Use of Property, Facilities, and Equipment

(15 Programs) Programs which provide for the loan of, use of, or access to federal facilities or property wherein the federally owned facilities or property do not remain in the possession of the recipient of the assistance.

Provision of Specialized Services

(92 Programs) Programs which provide federal personnel directly to perform certain tasks for the benefit of communities or individuals. These services may be performed in conjunction with nonfederal personnel, but they involve more than consultation, advice, or counseling.

Advisory Services and Counseling

(74 Programs) Programs which provide federal specialists to consult, advise, or counsel communities or individuals to include conferences, workshops, or personal contacts. This may involve the use of published information, but only in a secondary capacity.

Dissemination of Technical Information

(88 Programs) Programs which provide for the publica-

tion and distribution of information or data of a specialized or technical nature frequently through clearinghouses or libraries. This does not include conventional public information services designed for general public consumption.

Training

(46 Programs) Programs which provide instructional activities conducted directly by a federal agency for individuals not employed by the federal government.

Investigation of Complaints

(38 Programs) Federal administrative agency activities that are initiated in response to requests, either formal or informal, to examine or investigate claims of violations of federal statutes, policies, or procedure. The origination of such claims must come from outside the Federal government.

Federal Employment

(7 Programs) Programs which reflect the government-wide responsibilities of the Office of Personnel Management in the recruitment and hiring of federal civilian agency personnel.

While we do understand that most of you will be interested primarily in the Financial aspects do not overlook all the non-financial services that Uncle Sam can provide.

There are more than 1500 programs which are managed by 57 different agencies.

Because each agency handles such a large number of programs it is critical when dealing with any of these agencies that you follow the rules of Grant Seeking etiquette discussed later.

Types of Programs Available Through State and Federal Agencies

Free Money: Usually through direct grants that do not have to be paid back.

Business Consulting: Free management advice is offered on almost every business subject by the Department of Economic Development to minimize new business start-up management costs. Most people think they know everything about their product and probably do, but most people know little about business start-up and management.

Management Training: Most states will assign specialists to work with a new business with one-on-one management training. Do not overlook this. Sometimes a single piece of critical advice can save you thousands of dollars.

Employee Training Assistance: This program provides FREE MONEY to train employees. FREE MONEY is also available to send employees to school.

Research & Development Grants: FREE MONEY is available to attract high-tech related companies.

Program Consultants: States have highly trained management consultants who will locate federal grant programs and help you through the application process.

Venture Capital Financing: This method can provide FREE MONEY in the sense you wouldn't have to pay it back. You would, however, probably have to give up part of the ownership of your business in order to receive financing. Most states have their own venture capital finance teams that invest in high risk businesses.

Grants for Women & Minorities: Grants are available in most states for women or minorities who want to start a business. Most of these will be under specific programs from the federal government. At some point your state applied for and received a grant for minority business interests. You would need to locate that program at a federal level and then apply to it at the state level.

Low Interest Loans: The states will also make direct loans at low interest, or even co-sign a commercial bank loan. If a state co-signs a loan for you, it may subsidize your interest and reduce an already low-interest rate lower yet.

Small Business Assistance

Anyone thinking about going into business for themselves, or wanting to expand an existing business should rush for the world's largest "one-stop-money-shop" where FREE MONEY to start or expand a business is being held for you by the federal government.

It sounds absolutely incredible that people living right here in the United States of America wouldn't know that each year the world's largest source of free business helps deliver:

- Over $30 billion dollars in free grants and low-interest loans

- Over one-half trillion dollars in procurement contracts

- Over $32 billion dollars in FREE consulting and research grants

---

With an economy that remains unpredictable, and a need for even greater economic development on all fronts, the Federal government is more willing than it ever has been before to give you the money you need to own your own business and become your own boss!

In spite of the perception that people should not look to the government for help, the great government give-away programs have remained so incredibly huge that if each of the approximately 8 million businesses applied for an equal share, they would each receive over $70,000.

Most people never apply for a FREE GRANT because they somehow feel it isn't for them, feel there's too much red-tape, or simply don't know who to contact. The fact is, however, that peo-

The Federal government is more willing than ever to give you the money you need to own your own business.

ple from all walks of life do receive FREE GRANT MONEY and other benefits from the government, and you should also.

As with all grant seeking, the key to obtaining grants is preparation and persistence. Preparation means identifying programs that are available, and then determining if you fall within their restrictions.

The key to obtaining grants is preparation and persistence.

Be persistent. As you contact different agencies for grant money, learn not to accept "no" as a final answer. There are so many new programs being offered each year that often an agency's own employees won't be aware they are offering the one you ask about. If being persistent doesn't help, get in touch with your congressman and let them track down a program that meets your needs.

Education

More than $17 billion in financial aid is available for students each year, according to the College Board Scholarship Service. Although you don't have to be poor to receive aid, you have to prove you need it. Most students receive different types of financial aid. Grants (aid given without condition of return), loans and work-study programs are available. Many institutions offer grants, aids and work-study loans based on demonstrated need, not on past or present family income. Demonstrated need is the difference between what an education actually costs and how much a family can legitimately contribute toward a student's education. To qualify, fill out all aid forms at the college of your choice.

Types of Loans & Grants

The U. S. Department of Education offers several student financial aid programs. Many are grants which do not have to be repaid.

Pell Grants

Pell Grants are awards to help undergraduates pay for their education after high school. For many students these grants provide a "foundation" of financial aid, to which aid from other federal and non-federal sources may be added. Unlike loans, grants don't have to be paid back.

Pell Grant — doesn't have to be paid back

Pell Grants are:

• Free gifts--thus, no repayment

• For undergraduates only

• For part-time or full-time students

• Usually limited to 5 full years of study

Supplemental Education Opportunity Grants

**SEOG —
FREE gift loan**

A Supplemental Educational Opportunity Grant (SEOG) is an award to help you pay for your education after high school. It is for undergraduate students with exceptional financial need (priority is given to Pell Grant recipients). The grant does not have to be paid back.

- Free gifts–thus, no repayment

- For undergraduates only

- A campus-based program

- Awarded based on need and availability of funds

You can obtain up to $4,000 per year, depending on your need, the availability of SEOG funds at your school, and the amount of additional aid you are receiving.

Different schools set different deadlines. Deadlines are usually early in each calendar year, so apply as soon as possible. Find out what the deadlines are by checking with the financial aid administrator at your school.

**Perkins —
low-interest
loan**

Perkins Loans

The National Direct Student Loan has been renamed the Perkins Loan as a memorial to Carl D. Perkins, the late chairman of the House of Education and Labor Committee, for his support of public education and desire for a program of direct federal loans to students. The Perkins Loan is a low-interest loan to help you pay for your education after high school. These loans are for both undergraduate and graduate students and are offered through a school's financial aid office. Check with your school financial administrator to determine if your school takes part in the Perkins Loan program.

• Must be repaid.

• Are for undergraduate and graduate students

• Are offered through a campus-based program

• Are based on need and availability of funds

Borrow up to:
$4,500
$9,000
$18,000

Depending on your financial need, the availability of Perkins Loan funds at your school and the amount of additional aid you are receiving, you may borrow up to—

• $4,500, if you're enrolled in a vocational program or have completed less than two years of a program leading to a bachelor's degree.

• $9,000, if you're an undergraduate student who has already completed two years of study toward a bachelor's degree and has achieved third-year status.

• $18,000 for graduate or professional study.

Each school usually has a deadline early in the calendar year, so apply as soon as possible.

Government Student Loans

A Guaranteed Student Loan (GSL) is a low-interest loan offered by a lender such as a bank, credit union or savings and loan association to help you pay for your education after high school. These loans are insured by the guarantee agency in your state and reinsured by the federal government. Guaranteed Student Loan borrowers must:

GSL —
low interest
loan

• Repay their loans

• Be undergraduate or graduate students

• Be enrolled at least part time

• Apply for a Pell Grant

Depending on your need, you may borrow up to—

• $2,625 per year, if you're a first- or second-year under gradu-ate student.

• $4,000 per year, if you have completed two years of study and achieved junior status.

• $7,500 per year, if you're a graduate student.

You can't borrow more than the cost of education at your school, minus any other financial aid you receive. Remember, all GSL applicants must show financial need, and in some cases, the amount of need may limit the size of the GSL.

You should begin looking for a lender as soon as you are accepted by your school. After you submit your application to a lender and the lender agrees to fund the loan, it usually takes four to six weeks to get your loan approved by the guarantee agency. Consequently, allow yourself as much time as possible to complete the application process.

PLUS loans — borrowers do not have to show need

PLUS Loans

PLUS loans are for parent borrowers; SLS's are for students. Both loans provide additional funds for educational expenses and are offered by a lender such as a bank, credit union or savings and loan association.

PLUS enables parents to borrow up to $4,000 per year, to a total of $20,000, for each child who is enrolled at least part-time and is a dependent student. Under SLS, graduate students and independent undergraduates may borrow up to $4,000 per year, to a total of $20,000. This amount is in addition to the GSL limits.

The application process is the same as for a GSL. However, PLUS and SLS borrowers do not have to show need and may have to undergo a credit analysis. The guarantee agency in your state may charge an insurance premium of up to three percent of the loan principal. This premium must be deducted proportionately from each loan disbursement made to you. There is no origination fee for these loans.

SLS and PLUS borrowers must begin repaying interest within 60 days after the loan is disbursed, unless the lender agrees to let the interest accumulate until the deferment ends. SLS borrowers get the same deferments as GSL borrowers. However, under SLS, the deferments apply only to loan principal. PLUS deferments are much more limited and apply only to principal. For more information about specific repayment and deferment conditions for SLS and PLUS loans, contact your financial aid administrator, lender or the guarantee agency in your state.

If you are having difficulty finding a lender, then contact your state guarantee agency. It is the best source of information on the GSL, PLUS and SLS programs in your state. Banks and other lenders take part voluntarily in these programs and lend out their own money. While the Department of Education encourages lenders to provide student loans, it can't dictate the policies of a lending institution as long as those policies don't discriminate based on the applicant's race, religion, national origin, sex, age, marital status, handicap or financial situation.

Many of the rights and responsibilities of GSL borrowers also apply to PLUS and SLS borrowers. Lenders will also inform you of any refinancing options available when you take out a loan. If you have a GSL, PLUS or SLS and need to borrow again, contact your first lender to make future refinancing easier.

College Work Study

The College Work-Study (CWS) Program provides jobs for undergraduate and graduate students who need financial aid. CWS offers an opportunity to earn money for your educational expenses.

College Work-Study:

- Provides jobs, so you can earn money for school

- Is for undergraduate and graduate students

- Is a campus-based program

- Awards jobs based on need and availability of funds

Your pay will be at least the current federal minimum wage, but also may be related to the type and difficulty of the work. Your total CWS award depends on your need, the amount of money your school has for this program, and the amount of aid you receive from other programs. If you're an undergraduate, you will be paid by the hour. If you're a graduate student, you may be paid hourly or receive a salary. No CWS student may be paid by commission or fee. You will be paid at least once a month.

If you work on-campus, you'll work for your school. If you work off-campus, your job will usually involve work that is in the public interest. Your employer will usually be a private or public non-profit organization, or a local, state or federal agency. However, some schools may have agreements with private-sector employers for CWS jobs.

Your school will set your work schedule. In arranging a job and assigning work hours, your class schedule, health and academic progress will be considered. Remember, the amount you earn can't exceed your total CWS award.

A school may use a portion of its CWS funds for part-time and less than part-time students. To find out your school's policy on this matter, contact the financial aid administrator.

You will receive a list of the amount and kinds of financial aid available, including information about CWS employment. In addition to the specified loans and grants listed above, there are several types of aid offered by individual states.

Grants for Women and Minorities

Throughout American history, women and minorities have continually struggled to obtain a fair and equal share of the American dream. Congress has realized this and numerous programs were put in place over the years to help give these large portions of our society a leg-up.

These programs are for the people that are hard-working and self motivated that have that burning desire to succeed. Most of the programs are designed to remove barriers and hurdles created by a person's situation whether it is culturally based or socio-economic.

Throughout Grant Seeker Pro™ you will find hundreds of programs that were created specifically to assist women and minorities.

Specific grant types include but are not limited to:

- Grants for College

- Grants for Business Start Up

- Grants for Existing Business

- Grants for Legal Assistance

- Grants for Single Mothers

- Grants for Minorities

> *In addition to the loans and grants listed, there are several types of aid offered by individual states.*

- Grants for Housing

- Grants for Youth Assistance

> The Following quote was taken right from your Grant Seeker Pro™ CD.
>
> "To stimulate technological innovation in the private sector, strengthen the role of small businesses in meeting federal research and development needs, increase private sector commercialization of innovations derived from USDA-supported research and development efforts, and foster and encourage participation, by **women-owned and minority small business** firms in technological innovation."

Under this specific program you can receive as much as $150,000 per year! The average grantor is $95,000 and there is currently $13,000,000 set aside for this year. This is just one program that can be found on the enclosed CD. Type in 11.550 into the program number box and hit "Go."

Under this specific program ...the average Grant is for $95,000...

Here is another program located on your Grant Seeker Pro™ CD: "To enhance and further the opportunity of Disadvantaged Business Enterprises (DBEs) to obtain accounts receivable financing for the performance of transportation-related contracts emanating from the DOT, its grantees, recipients, their contractors and subcontractors."

It is estimated that over 130,000 businesses were assisted through this program last year and even more will be assisted this year.

Here is one more program targeting women and minorities in business. From this program you can receive a $500,000 line of credit

"**Objective:** To enhance and further the opportunity of Disadvantaged Business Enterprises (DBEs) to obtain accounts receivable financing for the performance of transportation-related contracts emanating from the DOT, its grantees, recipients, their contractors and subcontractors.

Applicant Eligibility: The recipient of a line of credit must be a certified DBE, minority-owned business enterprise or women-owned business enterprise. All firms certified by the Small Business Administration as 8(a) firms are eligible to participate in the Lending program."

These are just three examples of programs funded by the US Government that are specifically for women and minorities. You can gain instant access to any of these programs by accessing your Grant Seeker Pro™ CD.

Housing Grants

As homelessness became an issue throughout the United States, the US government was forced to create programs that would assist this portion of our society.

From these programs evolved additional programs that were designed to assist low-to-moderate income families enjoy the privileges and pride that come with Home Ownership.

There are a variety of grant programs that are available for housing. These include programs to assist with down payments, home repairs and home purchase.

Over $3,000,000,000 (3 Billion) has been set aside this year for just the one program shown below!

> *You can move into a single family unit or a multi family unit and pay on 30% of the standard rent for that area. That is right—the Federal government will pick up the tab on the remainder!*

Objective: To assist very low, low-income, and moderate-income households to obtain modest, decent, safe, and sanitary housing for use as a permanent residence in rural areas.

There are grants such as the one following that can be accessed in your area to acquire free technical assistance and equipment to build your own home!

Objective: To provide Self Help Technical Assistance Grants to provide financial assistance to qualified nonprofit organizations and public bodies that will aid needy very low and low-income individuals and their families to build homes in rural areas by the self-help method. Any state, political subdivision, private or public nonprofit corporation is eligible to apply. Section 523 grants are used to pay salaries, rent, and office expenses of the nonprofit organization. Pre-development grants up to $10,000 may be available to qualified organizations.

Many times we hear that "you have to be a non-profit organization in order to apply for this funding." The above mentioned program is one such program but did you know that your Grant Seeker Pro™ CD can aid you in finding out who in your area received that funding? Now you know who has the money and you can apply directly to them for your grant assistance.

These are just two examples of the billions of dollars made available each and every year to assist everyday Americans in home ownership.

Did you know that there are billions spent by the federal government every year to help people with their rent? You can move into a single family unit or a multi family unit and pay only 30% of the standard rent for that area. That is right—the federal government will pick up the tab on the remainder!

"To make good quality rental housing available to low income families at a cost they can afford, the federal government will make payments directly to owners to supplement the partial rental payments of eligible tenants. Assistance covers the difference between the tenant's payment and the basic market rental, but may not exceed 70 percent of the market rental. The tenant's payment is between 25 and 30 percent of monthly adjusted income or 30 percent of market rental, whichever is greater."

Over 4.5 billion dollars will be spent in 2005 for this single program!

As you can see the Federal Government wants you to have a roof over your head. For those that are truly homeless there is assistance—you just need to know where to find it. Use your Grant Seeker Pro™ CD to locate these programs and more.

GETTING STARTED

The Written Word

There does not seem to be a clear consensus on the exact number of sections in a grant proposal. Even the government seems to differ from department to department. For that reason it is extremely important that you always acquire the grant packet for the specific program you are applying to prior to writing your grant. Despite these differences, most seem to have the same basic organizational strategies. They all have an introduction, a description of the need, a stated goal or objective, how you will accomplish your goal, a project evaluation, a budget, a history of your organization, future funding, supporting documentation and a conclusion. For our purposes, we are going to utilize a general structure suggested by the U.S. government.

The Statement of Need:

This will be the first sentence a potential funder will read. The statement of need can literally make or break the entire process. While this is not meant to scare you off, it is meant to advise you that a single sentence can be that important.

The statement of need is usually just one brief paragraph that puts your whole project into a nutshell:

> "To obtain funding for the ongoing breakfast program of the Hilltop Elementary K – 6th grade students."

The statement of need above is clear and concise. Notice we did not discuss any aspects of the how. We only stated our original idea. As long as this core idea fits into the agencies guidelines for assistance then you will successfully move onto the next steps.

The Proposal Summary: Outline of Project Goals

The proposal summary outlines the proposed project and should appear at the beginning of the proposal. It can be in the form of a cover letter or a separate page, but should definitely be brief -- no longer than two or three paragraphs. The summary would be most

...the initial impression it gives will be critical to the success of your venture.

useful if it were prepared after the proposal has been developed in order to encompass all the key points necessary to communicate the objectives of the project. It is this document that becomes the cornerstone of your proposal, and the initial impression it gives will be critical to the success of your venture. In many cases, the summary will be the first part of the proposal package seen by agency officials and very possibly could be the only part of the package that is carefully reviewed before the decision is made to consider your project any further. As you prepare the outline, always work from your original statement of need.

You need to select a fundable project that can be supported in view of the local need. Alternatives, in the absence of federal support, should be pointed out. The influence of the project both during and after the project period should be explained. The consequences of the project as a result of funding should be highlighted.

Agencies receive thousands of proposals throughout the year. For this reason your summary must stand out. Bring your passion and zeal into it. Solicit friends for ideas. Purchase a thesaurus and use words that will relay your passion to the reader. Most computer programs have a thesaurus built right in. Use it!

wrong	**right**
Our project would feed breakfast to 100 school children.	By funding our project 100 children in Central Elementary will receive a healthy breakfast which in turn will create a better learning environment throughout the day.

While the first example did explain what the project would accomplish, the second gave it more of a personal touch and provided more of an extended vision of what is accomplished. Not only will the children eat but they will also be better prepared to learn.

Regardless of the objective, you must provide a brief effective narrative that within a couple of paragraphs describes the need and what your project will do to alleviate it. For those individuals applying for new business funding, make sure that you include information about how the support will assist the community at large.

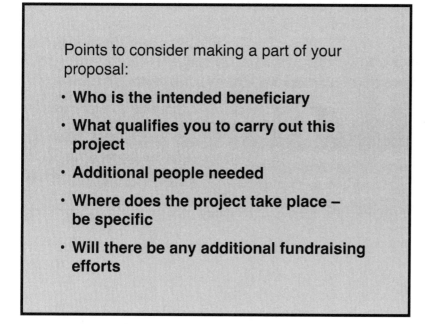

Points to consider making a part of your proposal:

- **Who is the intended beneficiary**

- **What qualifies you to carry out this project**

- **Additional people needed**

- **Where does the project take place – be specific**

- **Will there be any additional fundraising efforts**

Introduction:
Presenting a Credible Applicant or Organization

You will need to gather data about your organization from all available sources. Most proposals require a description of the applicant's organization. Here you will not need to be creative. Stick to the facts.

• Provide the founding date for your organization

• A brief biography of board members and key staff members

• The organization's goals, philosophy, track record with other grantors, and any success stories

• Data that is relevant to the goals of the federal grantor agency helps to establish the applicant's credibility

When completing this portion be sure to include articles about your organization. Any outside information either from other agencies or newspapers is extremely powerful. This allows the agency to read about what others are saying about you. What has your organization done in the past? Who have you helped?

A key point here is the funding received in the past from other agencies. The agency does not want to provide funding to a group that is floundering. The fact that you have received prior funding will show that there is an ongoing commitment to the objective of your organization and to the current request.

Always keep your vision in front of you. Tie your organization's accomplishments to the funding agency's policies. You can even use some of their wording. This way it will seem as though you are meant for each other. (Be careful not to copy verbatim.)

The Problem Statement: Stating the Purpose at Hand

The problem statement (or needs assessment) is a key element of a proposal that makes a clear, concise, and well-supported statement of the problem to be addressed. The best way to collect information about the problem is to conduct and document both a formal and informal needs assessment for a program in the target or service area. The information provided should be both factual and directly related to the problem addressed by the proposal. Areas to document are:

Describe the community and the beneficiaries that your project will serve.

➨ The purpose for developing the proposal. What kind of problem is it?. How is your project going to solve the problem or abate it?

➨ Describe the community and the beneficiaries that your project will serve and how it will serve them.

➨ The nature of the problem (provide as much hard evidence as possible). Provide statistics, newspaper clippings or even college papers that have been done on the subject. Do not overlook the college libraries as quite often college student will complete extensive projects on societal problems.

➨ How the applying organization came to realize that the problem exists, and what is currently being done. Do not be afraid to mention that other organizations are involved in the project. By drawing attention to it, you will actually increase your chances of getting funded. Most benevolent agencies like to see that others are involved. It adds another sense of realism to the project.

> *Review the resources needed, considering how they will be used and to what end.*

→ The remaining alternatives available when funding has been exhausted. Explain what will happen to the project and the impending implications. You will need to go into detail concerning potential funding later on. Will the organization be able to carry on after funding has been exhausted? Obviously if you are seeking funding for a one time use, such as sending inner city youth to a science camp, then you will not need to worry about this.

→ Most importantly, the specific manner through which problems might be resolved. Review the resources needed, considering how they will be used and to what end.

Here you will want to stay tied to your summary. You are explaining what it is that this project is going to accomplish. You are not out to solve all the problems in the world. Keep it local. While the money is important and it is what you are after do not make it all encompassing. By focusing more on the solution to the problem you will be seen as sincere and will increase your chances of ultimately getting funded.

Project Objectives: Goals and Desired Outcome

Program objectives refer to specific activities in the proposal. It is necessary to identify all objectives related to the goals to be reached, and the methods to be employed to achieve the stated objectives. Consider quantities or things measurable and refer to a problem statement and the outcome of proposed activities when developing a well-stated objective. The figures used should be verifiable. Remember, if the proposal is funded, the stated objectives will probably be used to evaluate program progress, so be realistic.

Program Methods and Program Design:
A Plan of Action

The program design refers to how the project is expected to work and solve the stated problem. Sketch out the following:

◆ The activities to occur along with the related resources and staff needed to operate the project (inputs).

◆ A flow chart of the organizational features of the project. Describe how the parts interrelate, where personnel will be needed, and what they are expected to do. Identify the kinds of facilities, transportation, and support services required (throughputs).

Create a flow chart and describe how the parts interrelate.

◆ Explain what will be achieved through 1 and 2 above (outputs); i.e., plan for measurable results. Project staff may be required to produce evidence of program performance through an examination of stated objectives during either a site visit by the federal grantor agency and/or grant reviews which may involve peer review committees.

◆ It may be useful to devise a diagram of the program design. For example, draw a three column block. Each column is headed by one of the parts (inputs, throughputs and outputs), and on the left (next to the first column) specific program features should be identified (i.e., implementation, staffing, procurement, and systems development). In the grid, specify something about the program design. For example, assume the first column is labeled inputs and the first row is labeled staff. On the grid one might specify under inputs five nurses to operate a childcare unit. The throughput might be to maintain charts, counsel the children, and set up a daily routine; outputs might be to discharge 25 healthy children per week. This type of procedure will help to conceptualize both the scope and detail of the project.

◆ Wherever possible, justify in the narrative the course of action taken. The most economical method should be used that does not compromise or sacrifice project quality. The financial expenses associated with performance of the project will later become points of negotiation with the federal program staff. If everything is not carefully justified in writing in the proposal, after negotiation with the federal grantor agencies, the approved project may resemble less of the original concept. Carefully consider the pressures of the proposed implementation, that is, the time and money needed to acquire each part of the plan. A Program Evaluation and Review Technique (PERT) chart could be useful and supportive in justifying some proposals.

Highlight the innovative features of your proposal that could be considered distinct from other proposals under consideration.

◆ Highlight the innovative features of your proposal that could be considered distinct from other proposals under consideration. There may be more than one organization fighting for the same money. For this reason you need to be seen as original and innovative.

◆ Whenever possible, use an appendix to provide details, supplementary data, references, and information requiring in-depth analysis. These types of data, although supportive of the proposal, can detract from its readability. An appendix provides the proposal reader with immediate access to details if and when clarification of an idea, sequence or conclusion is required. Time tables, work plans, schedules, activities, methodologies, legal papers, personal information, letters of support, and endorsements are all examples of appendices.

Evaluation: Product and Process Analysis

The evaluation component is two-fold: (1) product evaluation; and (2) process evaluation. Product evaluation addresses results that can be attributed to the project, as well as the extent to which the project has satisfied its desired objectives. Process evaluation addresses how the project was conducted, in terms of consistency with the stated plan of action and the effectiveness of the various activities within the plan.

Most federal agencies now require some form of program evaluation amonst grantees.

Most federal agencies now require some form of program evaluation amongst grantees. The requirements of the proposed project should be explored carefully. Evaluations may be conducted by an internal staff member, an evaluation firm, or both. The applicant should state the amount of time needed to evaluate, how the feedback will be distributed among the proposed staff, and a schedule for review and comment for this type of communication. Evaluation designs may start at the beginning, middle or end of a project, but the applicant should specify a start-up time. It is practical to submit an evaluation design at the start of a project for two reasons:

1) Convincing evaluations require the collection of appropriate data before and during program operations

2) If the evaluation design cannot be prepared at the outset, then a critical review of the program design may be advisable.

Even if the evaluation design has to be revised as the project progresses, it is much easier and cheaper to modify a good design. If the problem is not well defined and carefully analyzed for cause and effect relationships, then a good evaluation design may be difficult to achieve. Sometimes a pilot study is needed to begin the identification of facts and relationships. Often a thorough literature search may be sufficient.

Evaluation requires both coordination and agreement among program decision-makers (if known). Above all, the federal grantor agency's requirements should be highlighted in the evaluation

design. Also, federal grantor agencies may require specific evaluation techniques such as designated data formats (an existing information collection system) or they may offer financial inducements for voluntary participation in a national evaluation study. The applicant should ask specifically about these points. Also, consult the Criteria For Selecting Proposals section of the catalog program description to determine the exact evaluation methods to be required for the program if funded.

Future Funding: Long-Term Project Planning

Describe a plan for continuation beyond the grant period, and/or the availability of other resources necessary to implement the grant. Discuss maintenance and future program funding if program is for construction activity. Account for other needed expenditures if program includes purchase of equipment.

The Proposal Budget: Planning the Budget

Funding levels in federal assistance programs change yearly. It is useful to review the appropriations over the past several years to try to project future funding levels (see Financial Information section of the catalog program description).

However, it is safer to never anticipate that the income from the grant will be the sole support for the project. This consideration should be given to the overall budget requirements, and in particular, to budget line items most subject to inflationary pressures. Restraint is important in determining inflationary cost projections (avoid padding budget line items), but attempt to anticipate possible future increases.

Some vulnerable budget areas are: utilities, rental of buildings and equipment, salary increases, food, telephones, insurance, and transportation. Budget adjustments are sometimes made after the grant award, but this can be a lengthy process. Be certain that implementation, continuation and phase-down costs can be met. Consider costs associated with leases, evaluation systems, hard/soft match requirements, audits, development, implementation and maintenance of information and accounting systems, and other long-term financial commitments.

A well-prepared budget justifies all expenses and is consistent with the proposal narrative.

A well-prepared budget justifies all expenses and is consistent with the proposal narrative. Some areas in need of an evaluation for consistency are: (1) the salaries in the proposal in relation to those of the applicant organization should be similar; (2) if new staff persons are being hired, additional space and equipment should be considered, as necessary; (3) if the budget calls for an equipment purchase, it should be the type allowed by the grantor agency; (4) if additional space is rented, the increase in insurance should be supported; (5) if an indirect cost rate applies to the proposal, the division between direct and indirect costs should not be in conflict, and the aggregate budget totals should refer directly to the approved formula; and (6) if matching costs are required, the contributions to the matching fund should be taken out of the budget unless otherwise specified in the application instructions.

It is very important to become familiar with government-wide circular requirements. The catalog identifies in the program description section (as information is provided from the agencies) the particular circulars applicable to a federal program, and summarizes coordination of Executive Order 12372, "Intergovernmental Review of Programs" requirements in Appendix I. The applicant should thoroughly review the appropriate circulars since they are essential in determining items such as cost principles and conforming with government guidelines for federal domestic assistance.

Contact Tips
when dealing with officials.

Start making contacts by writing to specific agencies and requesting all necessary paperwork for the agencies funding criteria. Keep your initial request limited only to asking for applications and guidelines.

Remember, if your contact tells you they cannot help you with your project, just ask if you can be referred to an agency that can help. They may or may not know. Not every person knows what the government has to offer.

Don't burn bridges.

In order to establish the right contact it may take several letters. Remember don't burn any bridges in your pursuit, it may seem like you're getting the runaround, but the only way you can get anywhere with the government is to be friendly and offer a positive attitude to everyone you talk to; otherwise you may be dead in the water.

After you have established a contact, ask them to send information regarding their guidelines and applications for funding. Read them thoroughly to re-enforce any advantages you can use to further pursue your project.

When you find out that your project fits in their funding criteria, this is when you start on your proposal and letter of appeal. Submit to as many agencies as you can find. Being accepted by several agencies is not a bad thing.

To keep you from losing your call (or your cool) when trying to find an expert, keep the following guidelines in mind. Although most of them are common sense, when you begin to feel stressed, they will help.

Introduce yourself cheerfully.

Introduce Yourself Cheerfully: Your introduction will set the tone for the entire interview. Be cordial and enthusiastic, and give the person the feeling that this isn't just another phone call, but an opportunity for that person to be of great assistance.

Be Honest and Open: If you expect the person to be candid and open with the information you need, then you should expect to do the same. Would you help an individual that you felt was being deceitful? Do not expect others to.

Be honest.

Remember your "passion": Having a positive attitude when speaking to someone will go a long way. We have all heard in the business world that you must smile when on the phone. By doing this you are creating a positive frame of mind for yourself. Your cheerfulness and sincerity will be relayed to the person you are talking to and even the most difficult people will be more willing to assist you.

Be humble.

Be Polite & Humble: Never question another person's authority. If you feel that person is ill informed then politely ask to speak to someone else.

Be brief.

Be Brief: Be as clear as possible when explaining what you need. A long-winded explanation may bore the recipient of your phone call, so communicate your needs concisely. It will increase your chances of getting the information that you need.

Be complimentary.

Be Complimentary: Remember the old adage "Flattery will get you everywhere," it's true. Compliment the person on his or her expertise or insight. Do not be condescending or insincere. If a person has helped you in even a small way always say "Thank You"

Be Conversational: When you feel you have found your expert, don't overwhelm him or her with questions. First mention a few irrelevant topics to make the person feel comfortable. Being social puts you on a friendly basis and will make the expert feel like he just isn't being used, but is actually a human being.

Be polite.

A story was related to us once that went something like this:

The owner of a pots and pans company had been trying to sell his wares to a major chain of stores for several years. The best salesmen known were repeatedly sent to the CEO and buyers of this major chain, all to no avail. It was finally decided that they would have one more go at it. They called in their top salesman told him all the details. And sent him on his way.

Instead of hitting the CEO with his best sales pitch he simply sat and talked to the man. After an hour or so the conversation ended and they had not even talked about the pots and pans. As the salesman departed the CEO told him to stop by his secretary's desk and make arrangements to put his product in 100 stores!

The moral of this is to be polite. Treat the person like a friend. Do not be afraid to chit chat.

Return The Favor: You may find that you have information that may be beneficial to the expert as well. Share your information or even call back later during your research with information that the expert may find interesting.

Send Thank You Notes: This is perhaps one of the most over-looked items in the grant writing process. A short note showing your appreciation can help to ensure that you will receive additional assistance in the future. Keep notes of everyone you talked to and know their position. By strategically sending thank you notes you will build your own personal staff of experts that can be counted on to assist you in the future.

Send thank you notes.

Apply To More Than One Program: As mentioned earlier there is no rule that says you can't apply to more than one program. Some applications don't even ask you if you are receiving money from anywhere else. On the applications that do request this information you must answer truthfully. Many organizations like to see that others are also involved in the program. Simply applying to other agencies will actually increase your chances of being funded. Keep in mind that you may not be able to accept the money from all the departments that approve your application.

Apply to more than one program.

Give Them What They Want: Even though a question on the application may not seem logical to you, give the funder the answer that they are looking for. It doesn't help you to get angry and figh since the government will not change its question.

Starting Small Or Big? Depending on the program, you will need to be careful in saying how much money you need. Be sure you understand the maximum amount and the average amount of money given to applicants. We have tried to include all this information on the Grant Seeker Pro™ CD

Try Again: Never give up! If your application is rejected, it may have been a minor error on your part or even the government's. While it is not always possible to find this information out, you do need to try. Chances are if your application was rejected out of hand then you were applying to the wrong program in the first

Never give up.

place. If you were informed that your application was under review and consideration then it is usually easier to get an answer. Remember to always be polite. Do not whine and cry about being rejected because the officials are not going to change their minds. Simply asking why will usually get an answer. If it was procedural, then fix the problem and reapply. If someone else received the funding then try and find out what they did differently. Officials will be more helpful if they feel that you are being genuine. Incredibly enough some programs will turn you down just to see if you are serious about your project, so you must be persistent. This issue has been addressed by virtually every author on this subject. Funding agencies want to see the passion that drives the individual and what better way to show it than, if at first you don't succeed, try try again!

THE LAST RESORT

When the bureaucracy is stuck, use your representative: If you have found that the bureaucracy is having a problem with handling your paperwork in a prompt fashion, call your U.S. senator or congressperson to help give them a push. While it is very unlikely that you will ever talk to the actual senator or congressperson you must still be very professional when dealing with their offices. Be honest about the issues that you are having and even submit a copy of the proposal to them for review. This way, if they decide to assist you, they are armed with all the information that the agency already has. It is not recommended that you go straight to these offices with your proposal. Always start with the agency from which you are seeking funding. You will only use this step as last resort.

GRANT PROPOSAL SIMULATIONS

Lindbergh Chamber of Commerce

The Lindbergh Chamber of Commerce conducted a small business needs survey in April, 1996. Nearly 90 percent of the small business owners indicated that they needed more supervisory skills to improve their business operations. Nearly 78 percent indicated that they would attend supervisory training if it was offered in Lindbergh.

Southern New Mexico University (SNMU) Management Outreach Center

Once the project is implemented, the costs of sustaining the project will be minimal: approximately $30,000 per year to fund student help, telephone service, and equipment upgrades. Given the SNMU Management Outreach Center's sterling track record in raising funds to sustain projects ($300,000 in 1996), the staff is confident that it will be able to raise the necessary funds. The Center plans to seek funding from area corporations committed to diversity.

Grant Proposal Simulations

Welcome to the most important chapters of the Grant Seeker Pro™ manual. The following sections are actual grant proposals that were reviewed for approval. We are going to take you through each of the steps and critique each section individually. Once you have read through each of the following sections it is suggested that you write up your own practice grant proposal using the tips and techniques outlined.

While these simulations are certainly not all encompassing, they are without a doubt some of the best in the grant writing world. The processes shown here are based on actual instructional materials that are directly responsible for the acquisition of over $850 million dollars in grant funding. Yes, these materials are that successful. Non-profit grant writers and associations have paid hundreds of dollars to attend two-day training seminars based on these very materials.

...these simulations are...without a doubt some of the best in the grant writing world.

These simulations are based on two different organizations applying for a grant as a non-profit. Since many of you will be applying for grants and loans towards for-profit operations, keep in mind that the same rules will apply.

We will move through each lesson in as clear a manner as possible explaining each step along the way. Each step that the funding agency takes will be outlined in the following manner:

- ◆ **Criterion:**
  This statement will explain exactly what the agency expected to see in the proposal section being viewed. Throughout this exercise we will view ten criteria as set forth by the funding agency.

- ◆ **Response:**
  This section will show the response made by the competing organizations.

◆ **Critique:**

A short critique of each response showing the positive and negatives for that response.

◆ **Lessons Learned:**

A simple review of the preceding section.

◆ **Points:**

Earned by each organization for each criterion responded to.

Let's Begin

Grant Proposal Simulation 1

You are serving as an evaluator of proposals for one $100,000 government grant to teach supervisory skills to the owners of small businesses. On Saturday morning, you meet in a hotel conference room to select the winner from 42 entries. By noon, you have narrowed the field to 20. By 5:00pm, the field has narrowed to two organizations: the Lindbergh Chamber of Commerce and the Lincoln Department of Development. All of the evaluators are tired and cranky, but you all agree to make one more pass through these two proposals.

Lincoln Department of Development

The primary reason for the proposed activities is that the Lincoln Department of Development believes that education is a key element in the department's effort to continually improve economic development in Lincoln. Lincoln is committed to the use of supervisory training to help all businesses in Lincoln.

Criterion # 1:

The proposal clearly describes the need for supervisory training for small business owners (worth 15 points).

Critique	
Strengths	Weaknesses
Stated commitment while not in line with the criterion does show a high level of desire to succeed.	Does not answer the criteria. They did state their beliefs and commitments but that is not what the Request for Proposal (RFP) requested.
	The criteria emphasized the need for training of SMALL businesses in Lincoln and the Lincoln Department of Development stated that they were going to help ALL businesses. While this is admirable it is not realistic. Nor is it part of what the funders want to provide funding for.

Criterion # 1:

The proposal clearly describes the need for supervisory training for small business owners (worth 15 points).

Lindbergh Chamber of Commerce

The Lindbergh Chamber of Commerce conducted a small business needs survey in April, 2005. Nearly 90 percent of the small business owners indicated that they needed more supervisory skills to improve their business operations. Nearly 78 percent indicated that they would attend supervisory training if it was offered in Lindbergh.

Critique	
Strengths	Weaknesses
Note that they clearly and concisely established a need for the training through the use of statistics.	
There is no fluff here. It is simply stated.	

Lessons Learned

• Answer the question! This will be the underlying theme through this whole exercise and cannot be overstated. If an RFP provides a criteria no matter how ridiculous or unimportant you may think it is; you must answer it!

• Notice how easy it was to answer the criteria using statistics. Statistics and facts above all else are the easiest item in a proposal to evaluate. There can be no mistaking them and there is not much chance that they can be misinterpreted.

Avoid motherhood and apple pie statements. Do not make statements and promises that are ridiculously unachievable. "Lincoln is committed to use the supervisory training to help all businesses in Lincoln." This statement is something that is obviously not possible.

Answer the question! This will be the underlying theme through this whole exercise and cannot be overstated.

Criterion #1 Lincoln	Total Points Lincoln
0	0

Criterion #1 Lindbergh	Total Points Lindbergh
15	15

Criterion # 2:

The proposal clearly describes a schedule for analyzing, designing, developing, implementing, and evaluating the training (worth 10 points).

Lincoln Department of Development

If selected to receive the grant, Lincoln Department of Development will adhere to the following schedule:

Receive Grant . . . . .Week # 1

Analyze Needs . . . . .Weeks 02 – 08
   • Job Analysis
   • Task Analysis

Design Training . . . . .Weeks 09 - 12
   • Curriculum Guide
   • Student Guide

Develop Training . . . . .Weeks 13 - 23
   • Lesson Plan
   • Tests

Implement Training . . . . .Weeks 24 - 50

Evaluate Training . . . . .Weeks 51 - 52

Critique

Strengths	Weaknesses
Clearly and concisely answers the criterion.	Could perhaps have stated how they were going to evaluate the training. Ex: Evaluate training through use of survey.
The table breaks up the monotony of the proposal and yet keeps it very simple and clear. The table uses what is referred to as the 2 second rule. It can be read and understood in 2 seconds.	

Lindbergh Chamber of Commerce

Upon receipt of the grant monies, Lindbergh Chamber of Commerce will develop a schedule for the project. We plan to hire a consultant to assist us in developing the schedule and the training. Be assured that Lindbergh Chamber of Commerce recognizes the importance of having a detailed project schedule.

Criterion # 2:

The proposal clearly describes a schedule for analyzing, designing, developing, implementing, and evaluating the training (worth 10 points).

Critique	
Strengths	Weaknesses
None	Does not provide the requested information. You must answer the criteria!
	Failure to answer the criteria can display not only a lack of skill but also a lack of commitment.

Lessons Learned

Even the perception that you lack commitment can cause the loss of funding.

• Do not be afraid to use tables, charts or other simple illustrations to get your point across. Remember to keep them simple.

• Always provide requested info.

• Don't be casual in selecting grants to apply for. Even the perception that you lack commitment can cause the loss of funding. If you are lacking in passion do not waste your time or anyone else's.

Criterion #2 Lincoln	Total Points Lincoln
10	10

Criterion #2 Lindbergh	Total Points Lindbergh
0	15

Lincoln Department of Development

The following table shows the time commitment of key personnel who will be responsible for carrying out the proposed activities:

Key Personnel	Hours Committed Per Week
Executive Director	.05
Administrative Assistant	.10
Executive Board Representative	.02
Small Business Owner Representative	.01
University Liaison	.01
Training Consultant	.20

Criterion # 3:

The proposal clearly describes the time commitment of the key personnel who will be responsible for carrying out the proposed activities
(worth 15 points).

Critique	
Strengths	Weaknesses
Easy to read and answers the criteria. Abides by the 2 second rule in that the whole schedule can be taken in at a glance.	

Criterion # 3:

The proposal clearly describes the time commitment of the key personnel who will be responsible for carrying out the proposed activities.
(worth 15 points).

Lindbergh Chamber of Commerce

Key personnel who will be responsible for carrying out the proposed activities have committed a considerable amount of time for the duration of the project: the Executive Director will commit five hours per week; the Administrative Assistant will commit ten hours per week; the Executive Board Representative will commit two hours per week; the Small Business Owner Representative will commit one hour per week; the University Liaison will commit one hour per week; and the Training Consultant will commit 20 hours per week.

Critique	
Strengths	Weaknesses
Provides detailed explanation of who and how many hours.	This absolutely has to be in a table. This schedule is practically impossible to read. Once you do read it you have to go back and read it again to make sure you understand it. It breaks the two second rule. It could have stated how they were going to evaluate the training. Ex: Evaluate training through use of survey.

Lessons Learned

• While the detailed explanation will certainly suffice, not enough can be said about easy to read tables and charts.

Criterion #3 Lincoln	Total Points Lincoln
15	25

Criterion #3 Lindbergh	Total Points Lindbergh
0	15

...not enough can be said about easy to read tables and charts.

Criterion # 4:

The proposal clearly describes the involvement stakeholders (administration, staff, board members, small business owners, and the educational community) will have in the training activities (worth 10 points).

Lincoln Department of Development

All stakeholder groups will participate in the supervisory skills training project. The executive director will coordinate the project, ensuring that the project stays on schedule and produces desired deliverables and outcomes. The administrative assistant will provide desktop publishing support for training material development. The board, small business owner, and educational representatives will meet weekly as a steering group to guide the project through the five phases: analysis, design, development, implementation, and evaluation.

Critique	
Strengths	Weaknesses
Speaks to you in a strong active voice. Communicates to you what WILL happen. This shows that there is a sense of devotion to the project. The writer clearly sees the end result of their hard work.	

Lindbergh Chamber of Commerce

Participation of all stakeholder groups in the training project will be ensured. Coordination of the project to ensure that the project stays on schedule and produces desired deliverables and outcomes will be the responsibility of the executive director. Desktop publishing will be the responsibility of the administrative assistant.

Guidance of the project through the five phases – analysis, design, development, implementation, and evaluation -- will be ensured by a steering group. The weekly steering group meeting will be attended by the board, small business owner, and educational representatives.

Criterion # 4:

The proposal clearly describes the involvement stakeholders (administration, staff, board members, small business owners, and the educational community) will have in the training activities (worth 10 points).

Critique	
Strengths	**Weaknesses**
Answers the criteria.	Speaks in a passive voice. Stating their plan to ensure things will happen. This lacks passion and communicates a lack of interest in the task at hand. Where is the end vision?

Lessons Learned

*Write in
active voice.*

• Write in active voice: it's easier to read and shows that you can see the end result. Writing in an active voice is more likely to display your passion and enthusiasm for the project.

Criterion #4 Lincoln	Total Points Lincoln
10	35

Criterion #4 Lindbergh	Total Points Lindbergh
0	15

Lincoln Department of Development

The executive director has a vast amount of experience in plans and planning, from planning the department's **calender** to planning the daily **activites** of the staff. The executive director was involved in the PTE project, which, of course, was a huge success. The executive director has also been involved in other plans, and is recognized as one of the best planners in the field of economic development.

Criterion #5:

The proposal clearly describes the experience and training the project director has in strategic planning.
(worth 15 points).

Critique	
Strengths	**Weaknesses**
	Typographical errors on a document where they are asking for $100,000!!! What were they thinking? This is as inexcusable as it gets. You must use some type of word processing program. In this day and age of computers you must never have mistakes of this nature on any type of document being submitted for funding.
	What does PTE stand for? Who recognizes the executive director?

WLG
WORLD LEADERSHIP GROUP

150 North Hill Drive Suite #15
Brisbane, CA 94005
Main Phone: (650) 302-1002
ferdinandopilas@wlgdirect.com
www.WorldLeadershipGroup.com

Ferdinand Opilas
Regional Marketing Director

Code No. BE2791

Criterion # 5:

The proposal clearly describes the experience and training the project director has in strategic planning (worth 15 points).

Lindbergh Chamber of Commerce

The Lindbergh Chamber of Commerce executive director has had no formal education in strategic planning. However, the executive director has over 20 years of on-the-job experience in developing long-range (5-10 year) plans, helping over 100 small businesses. His planning contributions helped him earn a quality contributor award from the state association of chambers of commerce last year.

Critique	
Strengths	Weaknesses
While the statements made are not as strong as the previous proposal they are honest and verifiable. The director has received public awards for his work. This is something that in most cases can be verified with a simple phone call.	

Lessons Learned

• Typographical errors show a lack of commitment to the project. There is no excuse for not using a computer to pick up errors like this. You can even hire a proofreader to read your proposal for a penny or two per word. With this much money at stake the expenses incurred for ensuring correct spelling and grammar would be a mere pittance.

• Define acronyms and terms so that they can be verified. What is common knowledge to one group may be totally alien to the funders.

• Include only supportable statements. If an item cannot easily be verified then leave it out.

If an item cannot easily be verified then leave it out.

Criterion #5 Lincoln	Total Points Lincoln
0	35

Criterion #5 Lindbergh	Total Points Lindbergh
15	30

Criterion # 6:

The proposal provides evidence of a dedication to the project that indicates that the project will be successful (worth 10 points).

Lincoln Department of Development

Lincoln department of development personnel have read and heard quite a bit about the benefits of supervisory skill training and find the concept to be interesting. The grant will allow Lincoln to offer training that could be valuable in the future.

Critique	
Strengths	Weaknesses
	Once again they failed to answer the criterion. Where is the evidence?
	Need to take a more active role in the project. The words "interesting" and "could be" suggest that the applicants are not convinced of the projects viability.

Lindbergh Chamber of Commerce

The amount of time and money donated by the Chamber of Commerce, small businesses, and community representatives provides evidence of a dedication to the project that indicates that the project will be successful. We have raised over $45,000 in contributions from the community to be used for the project. Community volunteers have agreed to donate over 2000 hours to this project.

Criterion # 6:

The proposal provides evidence of a dedication to the project that indicates that the project will be successful (worth 10 points).

Critique	
Strengths	Weaknesses
Briefly and concisely answered the criteria.	Speaks in a passive voice.
Any time an organization can show matching support in the form of time or money they dramatically increase their odds of receiving the grant.	They may have been able to display this in a brief easy to read table.

Lessons Learned

*If you do not
have a thesaurus
then go out and
buy one.*

• Grant givers expect to see some sacrifice on the part of the grant writers.

• Any time that you have raised additional funding from other sources you need to make sure that it is discussed somewhere in the proposal. At some point most RFPs will directly request this information.

• Do not be lazy with your words. Choose words that indicate your commitment to the project. A good source of active voice words that show your enthusiasm can be found in the final chapter of this book. If you do not have a thesaurus then go out and buy one.

Criterion #6 Lincoln	Total Points Lincoln
0	35

Criterion #6 Lindbergh	Total Points Lindbergh
10	40

Lincoln Department of Development

The supervisory skills training program will help small businesses in Lincoln grow and improve by providing the small business owners with the knowledge, skills and abilities to effectively manage their employees.

Criterion #7:

In a single sentence, the proposal clearly describes the project mission. (worth 20 points).

Critique	
Strengths	Weaknesses
Followed the instructions perfectly.	
This is not the time to add flair. They want the project explained by you as you see it.	

Criterion # 7:

In a single sentence, the proposal clearly describes the project mission. (worth 20 points).

Lindbergh Chamber of Commerce

THE LINDBERGH CHAMBER OF <u>CMMERCE</u> WILL DEVELOP A WORLD-CLASS TRAINING PROGRAM. THE PROGRAM WILL BE VIEWED AS ONE OF THE BEST PLANS EVER DEVELOPED. LINDBERGH CHAMBER OF COMMERCE WILL RECEIVE AWARDS FOR THE TRAINING AND NATIONAL RECOGNITION.

Critique	
Strengths	Weaknesses
Ambitious	Did not follow the instructions which were quite clear. The funders asked for one sentence and one sentence only.
	Typographical error, the word "Commerce" is spelled incorrectly.
	Grandiose statement about what the are going to do.
	All capital letters. While it does stand out it is extremely difficult to read

Lessons Learned

• Follow the instructions. There is nothing more frustrating to professionals than people who cannot follow simple instructions. The first thing that any reviewer will look at is whether or not the applicant followed the instruction of the RFP.

• Use a minimum of 10-point type

• Never put sentences in all caps. While it does stand out it can be extremely difficult to read.

• Avoid grandiose, tired statements such as "world class" and "national center for excellence." They may sound great to you but chances are the funders have seen this too many times. Speak honestly from your heart and show your passion.

The first thing that any reviewer will look at is whether or not the applicant followed the instruction of the RFP.

Criterion #7 Lincoln	Total Points Lincoln
20	55

Criterion #7 Lindbergh	Total Points Lindbergh
0	40

Criterion # 8:

In 30 pages or less, the proposal clearly addresses all of the required factors defined in the request for proposal (worth 40 points).

✔ Required Forms
✔ Need
✔ Proposed Activities
✔ Evaluation Plan
✔ Allocations of Key Personnel
✔ Commitment to Broad-Based Participation
✔ Budget

Lincoln Proposal Table of Contents

Critique

Strengths	Weaknesses
Followed the instructions to the letter.	
Assembled their documents in the exact same order they were requested.	
Used the same terms as the RFP.	

✔ Required Forms
✔ Need
✔ Proposed Activities
✔ Evaluation Plan
✔ Allocations of Key Personnel
✔ Commitment to Broad-Based Participation
✔ Budget

Criterion # 8:

In 30 pages or less, the proposal clearly addresses all of the required factors defined in the request for proposal (worth 40 points).

Lindbergh Proposal Table of Contents

Critique

Strengths	Weaknesses
	Violated the page limit
	While changing the order and using your own terms are acceptable, why would you want to?

Lessons Learned

• Follow the rules.

• Use their terms instead of yours. Terms that are recognizable to the funder are more likely to score high. Also when they are comparing their index request to the applicants actual index they are able to clearly see and understand exactly where the information they seek is located.

• Emulating the RFP structure makes it easy for evaluators to give you a high score. Using their terms and phrases does not detract from the individualism of the proposal. There are plenty of other places in the RFP to show your style and passion.

Terms that are recognizable to the funder are more likely to score high.

Criterion #8 Lincoln	Total Points Lincoln
40	95

Criterion #8 Lindbergh	Total Points Lindbergh
0	40

Lincoln Department of Development

Criterion #9:

During the design phase, the Lincoln team will produce the following:

The proposal clearly describes the materials that will be produced during the development phase of the project (worth 15 points).

- ❏ 20 Lesson plans, (one per training session)

- ❏ 40 Examinations, (2 per training session)

- ❏ 60 Case studies (3 per training session)

- ❏ 20 Student handouts (1 per training session)

- ❏ Course evaluation sheet

Critique	
Strengths	Weaknesses
Clearly lists everything that will be produced during the process	

Criterion # 9:

The proposal clearly describes the materials that will be produced during the development phase of the project (worth 15 points).

Lindbergh Chamber of Commerce

The Lindbergh team will coordinate activities to ensure that all required training materials are produced on schedule. The consultant will focus on lesson and examination development. The educational representative and small business representative will work on case studies. The administrative assistant will work on student handouts.

Critique	
Strengths	Weaknesses
	Discusses the process of the items to be created. This is a common fault in grant proposals.

Lessons Learned

• Read the criteria closely. Did you really give them what they asked for? Had Lindbergh followed the instructions to the letter they would have easily fulfilled the criteria. In this particular instruction the funders did not care what the process was—they were only interested in the end result.

... they were only interested in the end result.

Criterion #9 Lincoln	Total Points Lincoln
15	110

Criterion #9 Lindbergh	Total Points Lindbergh
0	40

Criterion # 10:

The proposal clearly describes what performance indicators will be used to monitor the effectiveness of the program
(worth 15 points).

Lincoln Department of Development

The Lincoln team has identified the following performance indicators to monitor the effectiveness of the program:

◆ Sales volume/Income

◆ Employee turnover rate

◆ Employee absenteeism rate

◆ Customer satisfaction rate

Critique	
Strengths	Weaknesses
They have answered the criteria and the information is clearly written and easy to understand.	Could have been placed in a table.

Lindbergh Chamber of Commerce

With the benefaction of a practiced statistician, the Lindbergh contingent will employ absenteeism, turnover, sales, and customer satisfaction parameters. We really think it's important to do this. State-of-the-art analytical engines will be utilized to originate key data. This should give us some neat numbers to crunch.

Criterion # 10:

The proposal clearly describes what performance indicators will be used to monitor the effectiveness of the program
(worth 15 points).

Critique	
Strengths	Weaknesses
	This reads like it was written by two people. The language seems to adopt a pompous attitude.
	Once again avoid terms that can be seen as grandiose; "state-of-the-art".

Lessons Learned

◆ Write in one style/voice. Maintain consistency throughout the proposal. Any kind of sudden change in tone or voice may be seen as a lack of interest on the reviewers part.

◆ Avoid overly formal or informal words and phrases. Never try to be something you are not.

Never try to be something you are not.

Criterion #10 Lincoln	Total Points Lincoln
15	125

Criterion #10 Lindbergh	Total Points Lindbergh
0	40

**And the winner of the $100,000 Grant is...
Drum Roll Please!**

Lincoln Chamber of Commerce!

And the crowd goes wild!

Grant Proposal Simulation 2
Imagine the following:

Y ou are serving as a proposal evaluator. A large number of non-profit organizations and institutions are vying for a single $150,000 government technology grant. The purpose of the grant is to provide the winning organization with computer hardware, software, and training to allow the organization to establish an "innovative, highly interactive web site on the Internet to serve disabled citizens."

On Saturday morning, you meet in a hotel conference room to select the winner from 125 entries. By noon, you have narrowed the field to 10. By 5:00pm, you have narrowed the field to two organizations: Southern New Mexico University (SNMU) Management Outreach Center and the Piedmont Center for Disabled Citizens. All of the evaluators are tired and cranky, but you all agree to make one more pass through these two proposals.

Criterion # 1:

The proposal clearly and briefly describes the proposed project in the space provided on the application form. (worth 15 points)

This criterion could be considered the summary as defined earlier in the book.

Southern New Mexico University (SNMU) Management Outreach Center

We propose to establish a World Wide Web (WWW) site at which disabled American citizens (both students and practitioners) can receive advanced online education and training in management 24 hours a day.

Critique	
Strengths	**Weaknesses**
Addresses the purpose of the grant succinctly: "innovative, interactive web site on the Internet to serve disabled American citizens."	Doesn't define audience adequately: will this site be accessible to disabled citizens all across the country?
Grant writers typically write the summaries last, and in a hurry. What many don't realize is this is often the only opportunity to "stick the foot in the door." Grant proposals with well-written summaries will usually at least get read.	Doesn't establish the depth of need for this service. Who needs this service and why.
Suggests that the grant givers will get a lot of "bang for their bucks" (widespread access, 24 hour day training)	

Piedmont Center for Disabled Citizens

Based on a needs analysis performed of the region, the Piedmont Center for Disabled Citizens proposes establishing a World Wide Web site at which Piedmont Center clients can view legal and medical information, lists of resources and associated links, and news about upcoming events.

Critique	
Strengths	**Weaknesses**
Does a better job of defining the audience than SNMU.	**KEY**: Fails to address a key purpose of the grant: to establish an **interactive** site. This is a passive site. This alone could cause Piedmont to be rated less than SNMU overall. To be blunt, it really doesn't matter what the grant writers think about interactive sites; if they fail to meet the key grant giver requirements it is unlikely that they will receive the grant.
Suggests that need has been established.	
	The regional focus could hurt Piedmont – most grant givers want maximum return on investment. This does not mean that the grant must directly have a national focus, but the project structure or ideas should be portable to other organizations.

Criterion # 1:

The proposal clearly and briefly describes the proposed project in the space provided on the application form. (worth 15 points)

This criterion could be considered the summary as defined earlier in the book.

Lessons Learned

◆ Address the grant giver's purpose for giving the grant. You can have the best plans in the world. You may be the best person for the job but if you fail to specifically mention exactly what it is that the grant intended, then you are doomed. The requesters may indeed have a fabulous website planned that is the most interactive one ever built but that essential element failed to be conveyed.

◆ Define your audience/recipients/beneficiaries. Be very clear on this so that you can bring them to life. Make the grant givers see the beneficiary.

◆ Use the summary to "slip your foot in the door." This is what grabs the funder's attention. Remember, in a mere four hours we went from 125 potential recipients down to 10. How many of those 115 that were rejected actually had a better project planned than the ultimate winners?

◆ Target a broad audience or select a project that could serve as a model for other organizations. The more people you can help the better. Even if the grant is for local purposes, you must be sure to keep as many beneficiaries as possible involved.

◆ Establish the need for the project. Here Piedmont did an excellent job by stating, "Based on a needs analysis performed of the region." It shows they have done their homework and know their audience.

Even if the grant is for local purposes, you must be sure to keep as many beneficiaries as possible involved.

Criterion #1—Piedmont	Total Points—Piedmont
0	0

Criterion #1—SNMU	Total Points—SNMU
15	15

Southern New Mexico University (SNMU) Management Outreach Center

Upon entering the home page, the user reviews a list of management courses. Clicking on a relevant course title ("Providing Employees Feedback") the user accesses the course description, outline, and objectives; student reviews and ratings of the course; and a sample of the course content. The user elects to take the course, completing registration online. Soon the user is in the midst of a reality-based scenario in which she or he is providing feedback to a poorly performing employee. At each point along the way, the user must select a course of action and deal with the consequences.

Criterion # 2:

The proposal clearly describes a typical online exchange between a user and the proposed web site (worth 10 points).

Critique	
Strengths	**Weaknesses**
Most people who read this response find it intriguing. Successful grant proposals invariably capture the imaginations of the proposal evaluators. Remember that your proposal will often be competing against hundreds of other of proposals. Your proposal needs to stand out, and innovative content is more likely to do this than any other proposal element.	The course scenario could be a little too fuzzy for some proposal evaluators. It is good that the writers listed a sample course, but are the users presented multiple choice questions? Are graphics involved? A few sharp statements could help the proposal evaluators form a mental image of the project – a decided advantage.
Well-written and answers the criterion.	

Criterion # 2:

The proposal clearly describes a typical online exchange between a user and the proposed web site (worth 10 points).

Piedmont Center for Disabled Citizens

The user will enter a beautifully-designed home page, similar to the pages sponsored by major corporations and government agencies. Clicking easy-to-use icons and links, the user will effortlessly move through the site, stopping to read legal and medical information; news for the disabled, and other points of interest. The user will be able to download any or all site content for future use and reference.

Critique	
Strengths	**Weaknesses**
Well-written and answers the criterion.	Doesn't this approach sound like hundreds (thousands) of other web sites? For a $150,000 grant, the odds are extremely high that many of the other proposals will sound like this one. This statement is unlikely to capture the imagination of an organization giving a grant for telecommunication purposes.

Lessons Learned

◆ Capture the imaginations of the proposal evaluators. Make them visualize the experience. Take them on a tour through their own mind if you can. Explain the process step by step.

◆ Provide the evaluators with enough information so that they can formulate mental images of the project.

Criterion #2—Piedmont	Total Points—Piedmont
0	0

Criterion #2—SNMU	Total Points—SNMU
10	25

Provide the evaluators with enough information so that they can formulate mental images of the project.

Criterion # 3:

The proposal clearly defines the key project objectives.
(worth 10 points)

Southern New Mexico University (SNMU) Management Outreach Center

The key project objectives are:

- Analyze, design, and develop a World Wide Web (WWW) site at which disabled American citizens can receive advanced online education and training in management.

- Train SNMU management staff in the operation of the web site.

- Conduct a needs analysis of the center's telecommunications needs and address those needs.

Critique
Strengths
Bulleted format is easy to read. Begins with action verbs.
Weaknesses
The objectives listed are largely "process" or "enabling" objectives. Whether or not they state it, grant givers are typically looking for "outcome" or "terminal" objectives.
The matter is often confused by the nearly interchangeable use of the terms "objective," and "outcomes" in RFPs. When in doubt, provide outcome objectives or a mix of process and outcome objectives. If you list only process objectives you will typically find yourself repeating word-for-word the information contained in the description portions of your proposal.
Finally, the objectives are very broad, even vague. A little more detail could help these objectives dramatically.

Piedmont Center for Disabled Citizens

Criterion # 3:

The key project objectives are:

- Implement and maintain a World Wide Webs site at which at least 50% of Piedmont Center clients obtain information from their homes by the end of fiscal year 2005.

- Increase client awareness and understanding by disseminating useful information to clients in a timely manner on a daily basis by the end of fiscal year 2005. Awareness, understanding, usefulness, and timeliness will be measured by on-line surveys.

- Share lessons learned from the project with at least five other non-profit organizations by the end of fiscal year 2003.

The proposal clearly defines the key project objectives.
(worth 10 points)

Critique	
Strengths	**Weaknesses**
These are largely outcome objectives. Outcome objectives provide grant givers with a better picture of how their money will be spent, allowing them to determine the greatest return on investment.	A **potential** weakness could be failure to explain how the center derived their numerical targets, such as the 50% statement. If space permits, explain the reasoning behind such targets somewhere within the body of the proposal.
The use of numerical objectives and milestones offers the proposal evaluators some "meat to sink their teeth into." The authors of this course have seen many evaluators complain about the lack of measurable information in objectives.	

Lessons Learned

◆ When in doubt, use outcome objectives or a mixture of outcome and process objectives. Grant givers are typically looking for outcome objectives. They want to see the end results of their money.

◆ Establish numerical objectives and milestones when possible. Most people do not see generalities very clearly. Assign numbers and or specific time frames. These are things that the funders can in a sense touch and feel. They give the proposal more physical substance.

◆ If possible, explain the basis for numerical objectives within the body of the grant proposal. Show how you arrived at the numbers.

Assign numbers and or specific time frames. They give the proposal more physical substance.

Criterion #3—Piedmont	Total Points—Piedmont
10	10

Criterion #3—SNMU	Total Points—SNMU
0	25

Southern New Mexico University (SNMU) Management Outreach Center

Criterion #4:

The proposal contains a simple schedule
(worth 10 points)

	Analyze	Design	Develop	Implement	Evaluate
FY 02-2	Determine needs v	Design site v	– – – – – –	– – – – – –	– – – – – –
FY 02-3	Analyze requirements v	v	– – – – – –	– – – – – –	– – – – – –
FY 02-4	Analysis complete >	Design complete >	Develop site > v	>	Evaluate site design v
FY 03-1	– – – – – –	– – – – – –	Develop courses v	>	v
FY 03-2	– – – – – –	– – – – – –	v	>	v
FY 03-3	– – – – – –	– – – – – –	Development complete >	Implement courses >	Evaluate courses v
FY 03-4	– – – – – –	– – – – – –	– – – – – –	– – – – – –	v

Southern New Mexico University (SNMU)
Management Outreach Center

Critique	
Strengths	**Weaknesses**
A chart is almost always better than narrative for schedule and budget sections.	This chart fails the "two-second rule." Readers of tables and charts should be able to "see the big picture" within two seconds of looking at them. This chart takes much more than two seconds to figure out, and could easily confuse the reader.
	Proposal writers often run afoul by trying to get creative in the schedule and budget sections. Save your creativity for the project description sections. Stick with standard, familiar formats for schedule and budget sections.
	Because fiscal years differ from organization to organization, SNMU's use of fiscal year quarters is likely to lead to misinterpretation.

Criterion #4:

The proposal contains a simple schedule
(worth 10 points)

Piedmont Center for Disabled Citizens

	J	F	M	A	M	J	J	A	S	O	N	D	J	F	M	A	M	J	J	A	S
Analyze client needs	x	x	x																		
Design site		x	x	x	x																
Design site contents			x	x	x	x	x	x													
Develop site				x	x	x	x	x	x	x	x	x	x	x	x	x					
Develop site contents						x	x	x	x	x	x	x	x	x	x	x					
Implement site																		x			
Evaluate site and contents																		x	x	x	x
Improve site																		x	x	x	x

Critique	
Strengths	**Weaknesses**
The schedule passes the two-second rule: the evaluator can easily see the big picture within two seconds. This schedule uses a standard format, with calendar time for the horizontal axis and tasks for the vertical axis.	In this instance, a major problem for the proposal writer is determining how "simple" the schedule should be. Is this schedule too simple? It could be for some detailed-oriented evaluators.

Lessons Learned

◆ Use standard, easy-to-interpret formats and terminology for schedules and budgets

◆ Save your creativity for the description sections of the proposal

◆ Remember the two-second rule for charts and tables.

Use standard, easy-to-interpret formats.

Criterion #4—Piedmont	Total Points—Piedmont
10	20

Criterion #4—SNMU	Total Points—SNMU
0	25

Southern New Mexico University (SNMU) Management Outreach Center

Once the project is implemented, the costs of sustaining the project will be minimal: approximately $30,000 per year to fund student help, telephone service, and equipment upgrades. Given the SNMU Management Outreach Center's sterling track record in raising funds to sustain projects ($300,000 in 2004), the staff is confident that it will be able to raise the necessary funds. The Center plans to seek funding from area corporations committed to diversity in the workplace.

Criterion # 5:

The proposal identifies how the organization will obtain the financial resources needed to sustain the project after the grant money is spent. (worth 15 points).

Critique	
Strengths	**Weaknesses**
Ensuring that the costs to sustain the project are minimal and communicating this in the proposal is important – the landscape is littered with projects abandoned as soon as the grant money ran out.	In effect, this write-up asks proposal evaluators to "trust us, we'll get the money." That is a leap of faith that many grant-giving organizations are not willing to make. **Whenever possible, secure commitments/ pledges for out-year funding from other organizations and feature this commitment in the proposal.**
If your organization has not yet identified out-year funding, letting the proposal evaluators know that your organization has had a good track record in raising money for sustaining projects bolsters the proposal, provided that you can provide bullet-proof statistics to support your statements.	When evaluators reviewed this proposal section in real life, they questioned the organization's commitment to the project. If the organization was committed to the project, why hadn't they already begun the process of securing pledges for out-year funding?

Criterion # 5:

The proposal identifies how the organization will obtain the financial resources needed to sustain the project after the grant money is spent. (worth 15 points).

Piedmont Center for Disabled Citizens

Once the web site is fully implemented in September 2005, the costs of sustaining the project will be $40,000 annually (for salaries, telephone service, and equipment upgrading). Four corporations headquartered in the Piedmont service region have each pledged to contribute $10,000 per year to sustain the site during out-years:

❏ Charlotte Containex Group, Charlotte, SC

❏ Terra Firma Environmental Consulting, Columbia, SC

❏ Eastinghome Corporation, Columbia SC

❏ Joyce-Art Industries, Clemson, SC

Critique	
Strengths	**Weaknesses**
Having secured solid commitments for out-year funding is a major strength. Listing the supporting organizations in the proposal shows the proposal evaluator that support for and commitment to the project extends beyond the proposal-writing organization.	This write-up could be strengthened by listing contacts at each of the corporations, such as "Jane Smith, Human Resources Manager, (555) 555-5555."

Lessons Learned

◆ Avoid the "trust us" approach to out-year funding. While a good track record is extremely important, all of the money that was raised previously went for other purposes. You must address the issue of how this project is to be carried out. If it is going to generate its own income, then address that it will be self-sustaining and what the projected incomes are.

◆ Secure as much out-year funding/support as possible and list this along with the names addresses and phone numbers of the agencies or corporations providing the money. While these individuals may never be called, just the presence of the names and phone numbers will provide additional substance to the proposal.

Avoid the "trust us" approach.

Criterion #5—Piedmont	Total Points—Piedmont
15	35

Criterion #5—SNMU	Total Points—SNMU
0	25

Criterion # 6:

The proposal lists the organizational personnel who will work on the project, their titles, their education and experience, their project roles, and how much of their time will be devoted to the project (worth 10 points).

Southern New Mexico University (SNMU) Management Outreach Center

Project Member	Organization Title	Education	Experience	Project Role	Percent of work-time devoted to project
Joyce Watkins	Director, Outreach Services	PhD, Mgt. Univ. of Arizona	10 years operating outreach programs	Project Leader	25%
James Herlihy	IT Specialist	MS, IT Univ. of New Mexico	15 years in information technology	Webmaster	50%
Yvette Baca	Associate Professor	PhD, Mgt. Univ. of Michigan	10 years teaching experience	Curriculum Developer	25%
Tony Alston	Graduate Student	MS, Mgt. PhD candidate	5 years instructional technology experience	Instructional Technologist	50%

Southern New Mexico University (SNMU) Management Outreach Center

Critique	
Strengths	**Weaknesses**
In a limited amount of space, the proposal writers addressed the entire "laundry" list. Typically, proposal evaluators will approach laundry list criteria with a checklist mentality: does the proposal list all of the requested elements or not?	The proposal writer could strengthen this section by putting a little more information under project role, perhaps the most important category under this criterion.
The table is easy to read.	
The composition of the team reflects diversity.	

Criterion # 6:

The proposal lists the organizational personnel who work on the project; their titles; their education and experience; their project roles, and how much of their time will be devoted to the project (worth 10 points).

Piedmont Center for Disabled Citizens

Note: The attached resumes contain the organizational titles, education, and experience of the project team members.

- Amanda Jones, Project Director, 25% of time
- Ralph Smith, Webmaster, 50% of time
- Lakeesha Grant, Content Coordinator, 50% of time
- Mary England, Home Trainer, 75% of time
- Kevin Graham, Volunteer DAV, 100% of time

Critique
Strengths
The composition of the team reflects diversity.
Weaknesses
It appears that the proposal writers hit the "space panic button" when faced with the laundry list. One of the greatest challenges (perhaps the greatest challenge) in grant writing is saying all that needs to be said in an extremely limited amount of space. Exacerbating the problem is that more and more RFPs are restricting the overall length of proposals.
The writers of this proposal addressed the problem by including attachments, a serious mistake. Attachments make it difficult for the evaluator to check off the laundry list. Also, attachments are easily separated from the proposal and can be easily lost.

Lessons Learned

- As a rule of thumb, never include attachments of any kind unless specifically requested/allowed to do so. As stated above, it is too easy for them to get separated from the proposal especially when not requested. No one will know to look for them and the proposal may seem lacking.

- Use tables to address laundry list criteria. Remember to keep all tables simple and easy to quickly digest. Do not oversimplify since you will not be dealing with any fourth graders. (At least we hope not.)

Never include attachments of any kind unless requested/allowed to do so.

Criterion #6—Piedmont	Total Points—Piedmont
0	35

Criterion #6—SNMU	Total Points—SNMU
10	35

Criterion # 7:

The proposal clearly defines how the organization will measure the success of its project (worth 10 points).

Southern New Mexico University (SNMU) Management Outreach Center

The SNMU Management Outreach Center has set the following success measures for the project by the end of FY 2005:

◆ Positive online feedback from users (the site will have an open feedback forum)

◆ Positive feedback from employers on an annual paper-and-pencil survey

◆ Heavy utilization of the site as measured by the number of hits

Critique	
Strengths	**Weaknesses**
Including employer feedback helps to ensure the grant givers that they will get return on their investment.	**The success measures are vague (particularly the last measure), anecdotal (on-line feedback), and of questionable value (site hits).** Winning proposals list success measures that are as reliable, concise, relevant and quantifiable as possible.
	Most grant givers recognize that grant writers are not fortune tellers. However, grant givers are not interested in funding a project in **search** of a purpose.

Piedmont Center for Disabled Citizens

The Piedmont Center for Disabled Citizens has identified the following success measures for the project by the end of FY 2005:

◆ At least 50% of Piedmont Center clients obtain information from their homes by the end of FY 2005.

◆ Site information is updated on a daily basis.

◆ A statistically valid sample of clients rate the value of the site at 6.0 or higher (on a 10 point scale) on an online survey.

◆ Have shared project lessons learned with at least five other non-profit organizations by the end of FY 2005.

Criterion # 7:

The proposal clearly defines how the organization will measure the success of its project (worth 10 points).

Critique	
Strengths	**Weaknesses**
The success measures involve reliability (statistically valid survey), conciseness, relevance (non-anecdotal client feedback), and quantification (all of the objectives are quantifiable).	If space allows, the proposal writers could strengthen this section by discussing the logic behind the numerical values (such as 50%).
Will the relevance of these measures hold up through the passage of time? Perhaps, not, but they collectively make a solid attempt.	

Lessons Learned

Numbers are tangible values to the giver.

◆ Avoid vague, anecdotal, and irrelevant success measures.

◆ Ensure that your success measures are as reliable, concise, relevant, and quantified as possible. Again by assigning specific values you make the project more substantive. Numbers are tangible values to the giver.

Criterion #7—Piedmont	Total Points—Piedmont
10	45

Criterion #7—SNMU	Total Points—SNMU
0	35

Southern New Mexico University (SNMU) Management Outreach Center

The project will focus on delivering fundamental management training (such as leading, organizing, planning, and controlling), allowing broad participation not only by a diverse group of users (practitioners and students), but by other educational institutions and organizations as well. We plan to share not only our lessons learned in project development, but the actual site itself, establishing links to other distance training and education programs. In addition, upon request, we will assist other organizations in site setup, a relatively simple process due to the portability of the project.

Criterion # 8:

The proposal defines the applicability of the project to other organizations (worth 10 points).

Critique	
Strengths	**Weaknesses**
The proposal writers did a credible job of defining the multiple applications of this site outside of the organization.	If space permits, this could be strengthened by including the names of institutions and organizations that have expressed interest in the project.
Whether RFPs specifically ask for applicability or not, always work it into the body of the proposal.	

Criterion # 8:

The proposal defines the applicability of the project to other organizations (worth 10 points).

Piedmont Center for Disabled Citizens

By the end of FY 2005, the Piedmont Center for Disabled Citizens will have shared learned project lessons with at least five other non-profit organizations.

Critique	
Strengths	**Weaknesses**
The quantification certainly suggests a willingness to share.	**The write-up simply does not answer the question.** The criterion asks the proposal writers to establish applicability to other organizations. Instead, the writers give a success measure.

Lessons Learned

◆ In the body of your proposal always establish the applicability of your project to other organizations: How you can help each other. If your project is going to assist others, then you need to state who and how they are to be helped.

◆ Demonstrate a desire to share your results and lessons learned. By doing this, you reduce future overall funding needed by other organizations.

◆ Address the criteria! This cannot be overstated. If a criteria is laid out before you, then you must state how you plan to address it.

Address the criteria! This cannot be overstated.

Criterion #8—Piedmont	Total Points—Piedmont
0	45

Criterion #8—SNMU	Total Points—SNMU
10	45

Criterion # 9:

The proposal lists the project goals (worth 10 points).

Southern New Mexico University (SNMU) Management Outreach Center

The SNMU Management Outreach Center uses the term, "objective" instead of "goal." The objectives for the project are listed under Section III, "Objectives."

Critique	
Strengths	**Weaknesses**
None	Are the terms "objective" and "goal" synonymous? In most organizations and institutions they are not. The simple fact that the grant givers asked for goals and objectives in different sections of the RFP should have clued the proposal writers to deliver objectives AND goals. This write-up seems to suggest that the grant writers know what they are talking about and the grant givers do not. Obviously, this is a losing strategy.
	Cross-referencing turns off a lot of proposal evaluators (they tire of flipping back and forth in your proposal). Cross-reference only if space is at a premium and the RFP is asking for redundant information.

Piedmont Center for Disabled Citizens

The strategic goals for the project are:

◆ Improve client quality of life by providing them easier access to important information.

◆ Improve the quality of life of disabled citizens on a national basis by sharing the program with other organizations.

Criterion # 9:

The proposal lists the project goals (worth 10 points).

Critique	
Strengths	**Weaknesses**
These meet the criteria for strategic goals – simple, big picture-oriented, customer-focused, and important.	None
Are there too few goals? The authors believe the two goals listed above are powerful by themselves – adding additional goals would diminish their impact.	

Goals should be simple, big picture-oriented, customer-focused, important, and few.

Lessons Learned

◆ If the grant givers ask for apples and oranges, don't give them all apples and argue that apples and oranges are the same thing.

◆ Cross-reference only if space is at a premium and the RFP is asking for redundant information; however ensure that the information is indeed redundant!

◆ Goals should be simple, big picture-oriented, customer-focused, important, and few.

Criterion #9—Piedmont	Total Points—Piedmont
10	55

Criterion #9—SNMU	Total Points—SNMU
0	45

And the winner of the $150,000 Grant is...
Drum Roll Please!

Piedmont Center for Disabled Citizens!

And the crowd goes wild!

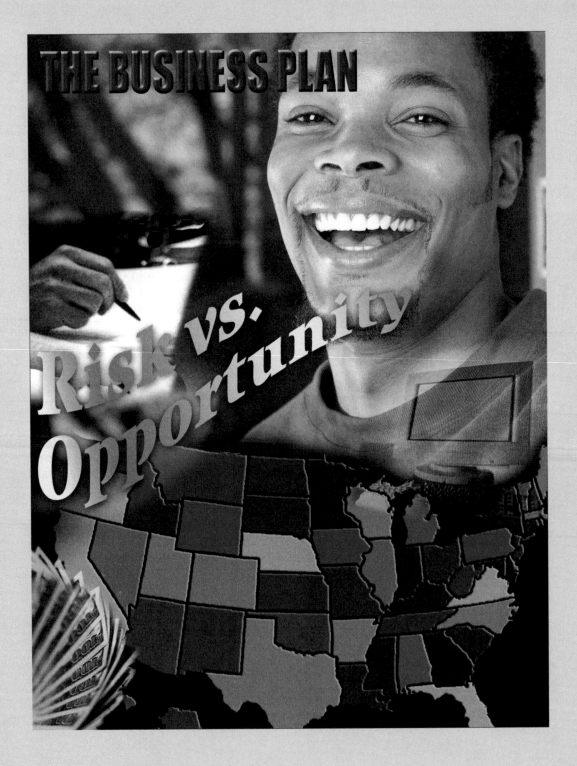

THE BUSINESS PLAN

Risk vs.
Opportunity

Business Plans

One of the most common requests we receive everyday is "Will you please send me an application?" When we ask what type, the answer is generally that they need an application for a "small business loan." When asked if they have completed a business plan, the answer is almost always "no." Most people wonder why they should put a lot of effort into a business plan if they are only going to be declined. The truth of the matter is, if you have a viable business plan in place ready to show the government bean counters, or the bank, then you are well on your way to success. We absolutely guarantee that if you do not have a business plan in place, then you will definitely be denied. You will be quite fortunate if you are not laughed out of the building.

Whether you are seeking loans or grants you will need a business plan. Without one you are wasting your time and everyone else's time when you ask to apply. This is where your Grant Seeker Pro™ CD comes in.

On your CD, locate the Business Plan section. Using this part of the program you will literally be able to print the perfect business plan. Your business plan will be modeled after the template that follows. All you need to do is fill in the blanks based on these instructions.

Executive Summary ─────────────

Mission

Company Overview

    Legal Business Description

    Strategic Alliances

Product

    Current Product

    Research and Development

    Production and Delivery

The Market

    Market Definition

    Customer Profile

    Marketing Plan

    Sales Strategy

    Distribution Channels

    Advertising, Promotion, PR

Competition

Risk/Opportunity

Management Team

Capital Requirements

    Exit/Payback Strategy

Financial Plan

    Assumptions

    Financial Statements

    Conclusion

Exhibits

Elements of a Business Plan

1. Cover sheet

2. Statement of purpose

3. Table of contents

I. The Business

    A. Description of business

    B. Marketing

    C. Competition

    D. Operating procedures

    E. Personnel

    F. Business insurance

    G. Financial data

II. Financial Data

    A. Loan applications

    B. Capital equipment and supply list

    C. Balance sheet

    D. Breakeven analysis

    E. Pro-forma income projections (profit & loss statements)

        - Three-year summary

        - Detail by month, first year

        - Detail by quarters, second and third years

        - Assumptions upon which projections were based

    F. Pro-forma cash flow

        - Follow guidelines for letter E.

III. Supporting Documents

        - Tax returns of principals for last three years

- Personal financial statement (all banks have these forms)

    - In the case of a franchised business, a copy of franchise contract and all supporting document provided by the franchisor

- Copy of proposed lease or purchase agreement for building space

- Copy of licenses and other legal documents

- Copy of resumes of all principals

- Copies of letters of intent from suppliers, etc.

Grant Seeker Pro™ guides you through a series of question and answer forms, provides step-by-step advice, and builds your final business plan for you.

Grant Seeker Pro™

Load Save View Exit Help

File : request

Business
We make [describe product, or service that you make or provide].

We provide daycare services to senior citizens in the Riverside area.

Our company is at the [seed, start-up, growth] stage of business, having just [developed our first prod hired our first salesman, booked our first national order].

In the most recent quarter, John Doe Company achieved a profit of $5,000. With the financing contemplated herein, our company expects to double that amount each quarter because we will be able to build new facilities and hire new employees.

In the most recent [period], our company achieved sales of [x], and showed a [profit, loss, break-eve With the financing contemplated herein, our company expected to achieve [x] in sales and [x] in preta profits in 19[xx] and achieve [x] in sales and [x] in pretax profits in 19[xx+1]. We can achieve this bec the funds will allow us to [describe what you will do with the funds, such as a) marketing for your new product, b) build or expand facilities to meet increased demand, c) add retail locations or others mean distribution, d) increase research and development for new products or to improve existing ones.

THE BUSINESS PLAN - WHAT IT INCLUDES

W hat goes into a business plan? This is an excellent question. In addition, it is one that many new and potential small business owners should ask, but oftentimes do not.

The body of the business plan
can be divided into four distinct sections:

❏ *The description of the business*

❏ *The marketing plan*

❏ *The financial management plan*

❏ *The management plan*

Addenda to the business plan should include the executive summary, supporting documents and financial projections.

DESCRIPTION OF THE BUSINESS

In this section, provide a detailed description of your business. An excellent question to ask yourself is: "What business am I in?" In answering this question include your products, market and services, as well as a thorough description of what makes your business unique. Remember, however, that as you develop your business plan, you may have to modify or revise these initial answers.

The business description section is divided into three primary sections. The first actually describes your business, The second covers the product or service you will be offering and the third is regarding the location of your business. Why is this location is desirable? If you have a franchise, some franchisors assist in site selection.

Description

When describing your business, generally you should explain:

- ❑ Legalities/business form: proprietorship, partnership, etc.

- ❑ Business type: merchandising, manufacturing or service

- ❑ What your product or service is

- ❑ Is it a new independent business, a takeover, an expansion, a franchise?

- ❑ Why your business will be profitable. What are the growth opportunities? Will franchising impact growth opportunities?

- ❑ When your business will be open (days, hours)

- ❑ What you have learned about your kind of business from outside sources (trade suppliers, bankers, other franchise owners, franchisor, publications)

Include a cover sheet before the description. List the name, address and telephone number of the business and the names of all principals. In the description of your business, describe the unique aspects and how or why they will appeal to consumers. Emphasize any special features that you feel will appeal to customers and explain how and why these features are appealing.

The description of your business should clearly identify goals and objectives and it should clarify why you are, or why you want to be, in business.

Grant Seeker Pro™

Load Save View Exit Help

File : request

Business Plan Wizard

Enter Your Company Name	John Doe Company
Date Month and Year of Issue	
Business Plan Copy Number	09098-08
Name of Point man in financing	John Doe
Title	Owner
Address	5555 Riverside Dr.
City	Riverside
State	CA Zip 95555
Phone	(555) 555-5555
E-Mail	jdoe@earthlink.com
Company home page URL	

This is a buisiness Plan. It does not imply an offering of Securities

---

Product/Service

Describe the benefits of your goods and services from your customers' perspective. Successful business owners know or at least have an idea of what their customers want or expect from them. This type of anticipation can be helpful in building customer satisfaction and loyalty, additionally serving as a good strategy for beating the competition or retaining your competitiveness.

Describe:

❑ What you are selling

❑ How your product or service will benefit the customer

❑ Which products/services are in demand; if there will be a steady flow of cash

❑ The uniqueness of the product or service your business is offering

The Location

The location of your business can play a decisive role in its success or failure. It should be built around your customers, be accessible and provide a sense of security. Consider these questions when addressing this section of your business plan:

❑ What are your location needs?

❑ What kind of space will you need?

❑ Why is the area desirable? the building desirable?

❑ Is it easily accessible? Is public transportation available? Is street lighting adequate?

❑ Are market shifts or demographic shifts occurring?

It may be a good idea to make a checklist of questions you identify when developing your business plan. Categorize your questions. As you answer each one, remove it from your list.

The Marketing Plan

Marketing plays a vital role in successful business ventures. How well you market your business, along with a few other considerations, will ultimately determine your degree of success or failure. The key element of a successful marketing plan is to know your customers -- their likes, dislikes, expectations. By identifying these factors, you can develop a marketing strategy that will allow you to meet their needs.

Identify your customers by their age, sex, income, educational level and residence. At first, target only those customers who are more likely to purchase your product or service. As your customer base expands, you may need to consider modifying the marketing plan to include other customers.

Develop a marketing plan for your business by answering the following questions. Be sure to include your marketing plan along with the business plan and ensure that it contains answers to the questions outlined below. Please note: Potential franchise owners will have to use the marketing strategy the franchisor has developed.

- ◆ Who are your customers? Define your target market(s)

- ◆ Are your markets growing? steady? declining?

- ◆ Is your market share growing? steady? declining?

- ◆ If a franchise, how is your market segmented?

- ◆ Are your markets large enough to expand?

- ◆ How will you attract, hold, increase your market share? If a franchise, will the franchisor provide assistance in this area?

◆ Based on the franchisor's strategy, how will you promote your sales?

◆ What pricing strategy have you devised?

Marketing plays a vital role in successful business ventures. How well the plan you develop markets your business, along with the management and financial management plans, will ultimately determine your degree of success or failure. The key elements of a successful marketing plan are to 1) know your customers -- their likes, dislikes and expectations, and 2) to know your competitors -- their strengths and weaknesses. By identifying these factors, you can better understand competitors and identify changes in the marketplace that can affect your bottom line.

The purpose of the marketing plan is to define your market, i.e., identify your customers and competitors, to outline a strategy for attracting and keeping customers and to identify and anticipate change. Your business will not succeed simply because you want it to succeed. It takes careful planning and a thorough understanding of the marketplace to develop a strategy that will ensure success.

Understanding the Marketplace

Generally, the first and most important step in understanding the market is to study it through market research. In the case of a franchise, the franchisor has developed a marketing program, so you will need to review the program he or she has provided. Look over the plan to determine what product/service you will offer and write a description. Even though a franchisor has described your product or service, it is a good idea to develop and write your own description because this process helps to reinforce your understanding of the product or service–a key variable in any successful marketing plan. In the description, outline what you feel are unique aspects, and explain how or why these elements will appeal to customers. Emphasize the special features that you feel are its selling points. These characterisitcs are what you will use to convince

Appendix I contains a sample entitled Marketing Plan and Marketing Tips, Tricks and Traps, a condensed guide on how to market your product or service. Study these documents carefully when developing the marketing portion of your business plan.

customers to purchase your product or service.

Next go over sales projections, determining if there is a demand for the product or service. In the case of a franchise, the franchisor will have developed the projections. Study this data to see how he or she arrived at these projections. This will help you to better understand how the marketplace operates relative to your product/service, and it can help you develop the skills necessary to identify and anticipate changes in the marketplace.

Start your own file on marketplace trends. Periodically review the data and look for shifts in the market. As changes occur, modify the marketing plan to coincide. In franchise operations, it is customary for the franchisor to update the marketing plan periodically to reflect changes in the marketplace and to keep the marketing program current.

A marketing plan should answer these questions:

- Is this product or service in constant demand?

- How many competitors provide the same product or service?

- Can you create a demand for your service or product?

- Can you effectively compete in price, quality and delivery?

- If a franchise, will the franchisor price the product or service to give you the projected profit?

Review your program to ensure that it answers these questions. If your plan doesn't answer the questions, it will need to be modified, or you will need to devise a strategy that will provide answers. When you are satisfied that you understand the program, how the market operates, and how to identify market shifts and trends, start writing the marketing section of your business plan.

Even if you adopt a program that has been developed elsewhere, it is your responsibility to promote your product or service by cultivating the marketplace, i.e., attracting and keeping customers. You can accomplish this aim by knowing your market, your customers, your competitors and your product/service. Don't rely solely upon the program provided by a franchisor or others. Gather and assess your own data using the techniques outlined in your plan. By analyzing this information, you will be well equipped to determine if your program is in line with competitors, and industry standards, and what adjustments are necessary to improve your overall success.

A sample marketing plan is attached as part of Appendix I. Study it carefully, then try to develop a similar program for your business plan.

Marketing Your Business for Success What Does a Marketing Plan Contain?

Many first-time business owners think that by simply placing an ad in a local newspaper or commercial on radio or television, customers will automatically flock to purchase their product or service. This is true to a certain extent. Some people are likely to learn about your product or service and try it, just out of curiosity. But hundreds, even thousands of other potential customers may never learn of your business. Just think of the money you'll lose, simply because you didn't develop an adequate marketing program!

Marketing is an essential part of business operations. And, oftentimes it determines how successful your business will be. What you as a potential business owner must do is maintain a thorough understanding of the marketing program and use it to extract advantages from the marketplace. Study the strategies and techniques until your understanding of the application allows you to get the results you desire. Remember, your aim is to not only attract and keep a steady group of loyal customers, but also to expand your customer base by identifying and attracting new customers and reducing risks by anticipating market shifts which can affect your bottom line.

To help you accomplish this goal, your marketing plan should include typical marketing strategies. The plan should especially include what marketers dub as the "4 Ps of Marketing" (PRODUCT/SERVICE, PRICE, PLACE AND PROMOTION). Review your plan. Make certain it contains the strategies listed below, and then determine how they are applied. Include a brief explanation for each strategy.

Describe the target market by

- age
- sex
- profession/career
- income level
- educational level
- residence

Identify and describe your customers (target market) by their age, sex, income/educational levels, profession/career and residence. Know your customers better than you know anyone—their likes, dislikes, expectations. Since you will have limited resources target only those customers who are more likely to purchase your product or service. As your franchise grows and your customer base expands, you may need to consider modifying this section of the marketing plan.

Identify Competition

- market research data
- demand for product or service
- nearest direct and indirect competitors
- strengths and weaknesses of competitors
- assessment of how competitors businesses are doing
- description of the unique features of your product or service
- similarities and differences between your product or service and competitor's
- pricing strategy comparison

Identify the five nearest direct competitors and the indirect competitors. Start a file on each identifying their weaknesses and strengths, advertising and promotional materials and pricing strategies. Review these files periodically determining when and how often they advertise, sponsor promotions, and offer sales.

Describe Product/Service

➡ describe your product or service

Describe the benefits of your goods or services from the customer's perspective. Emphasize special features–i.e., the selling points. Successful business owners know or at least have an idea of what their customers want or expect. This type of anticipation can be helpful in building customer satisfaction and loyalty.

Develop Marketing Budget

➡ advertising and promotional plan

➡ costs allocated for advertising and promotions

➡ advertising and promotional materials

➡ list of advertising media to be used

Operating an effective marketing plan requires money, therefore allocate funds from an operating budget to cover advertising, promotional, and all other costs associated. Develop a marketing budget based upon the cost of media, collecting research data, and monitoring shifts in the marketplace.

Describe Location (Place)

- description of the location
- advantages and disadvantages of location

Again, with the customer's perspective in mind, describe the location of your business. Describe its assets – i.e., the convenience, whether or not public transportation is accessible, and the safety aspects–street lighting, well-lit parking lot or facility, decor, etc. Your location should be built around your customers. It should be accessible and provide a sense of security. An advantage of purchasing a franchise is the franchisor oftentimes assists in site selection and decorating.

Develop Pricing Strategy

- pricing techniques and brief description of these
- retail costing and pricing
- competitive position
- pricing below competition
- pricing above competition
- price lining
- multiple pricing
- service costs and pricing (for service businesses only)
- service components
- material costs
- labor costs
- overhead costs

Although your pricing strategy may be based upon the strategy devised by others, study this plan and the strategies used by competitors. That way you will acquire a thorough understanding of how to price your product or service, and you can determine if your prices are in line with industry averages and what adjustments you can make.

The key to success is to have a well-planned strategy, establish policies and constantly monitor prices and operating costs to ensure profits. Keep abreast of changes in the marketplace which can affect the bottom line.

Develop Promotional Strategy

- develop an effective promotional strategy
- advertising media
- print media (newspaper, magazine, classified ads, Yellow Pages advertising, brochure)
- radio
- television
- networking
- business cards
- tee shirts, hats, buttons, pens

Develop a promotional strategy that uses various media and identify and monitor those that most effectively promote your business. Concentrate on developing material for those formats which clearly identify your goods or services, its location, and price.

Since financial institutions weigh the soundness of your marketing plan when deciding whether your business is a solid risk, it is important that you prepare and present credible marketing data that shows a need in the community for your business and demonstrates your ability to compete

Market Research

Strategies for Researching the Market

Researching your market is perhaps the easiest way to assess it. Market research does not have to be costly, nor does it have to be a complex process. It can be as simple and easy as surveying a cross-section of your consumers (focus group) to get opinions about the product or service you will be offering, or conducting a telephone or mail survey. One disadvantage of using the telephone or mail survey method is that the individuals you contact may not be interested in responding to a survey. Other market research techniques include analyzing demographic data, such as population growth/decline rate, age range, sex, income/educational level; brainstorming with family and friend and, focus group interviews. Whatever method you use, your focus should be on gathering enough information to determine who your potential customers are – their needs, wants and expectations. If there is a demand for your product or service, who are your competitors and how well are they doing.

Market research should answer questions such as:

▲   Who are your customers and potential customers?

▲   What kind of people are they?

▲   Where do they live?

▲   Can and will they buy the product or service you're offering?

▲   Are you offering the kinds of goods or services they want at the best place, the best time, and best amounts?

▲   Are your prices consistent with what the buyers view as the products' values?

▲   Are you applying the promotional programs in a way that will bring about success?

- ▲ What do customers think of your franchise?

- ▲ Who are your competitors?

- ▲ If a franchise, how does your operation compare with the competition?

Do not forego this process or stop halfway because you are not getting the desired results. This may be the only indication that you receive that you are going into the wrong business or that there is no market for your product or service. Don't be discouraged. You may simply need to modify your original plan.

A few of the benefits of market research are outlined below:

- ▲ Learning who your customers are and what they want.

- ▲ Learning how to reach your customer and how frequently you should try to communicate with them

- ▲ Learning which appeals are most effective

- ▲ Learning the relative successes of different marketing strategies in relationship to their return on investment

While market research may appear to be a tedious, time-consuming process, it is necessary if you want to be successful. Think of market research as simply a method of finding out what catches customers' attention by observing their actions and drawing conclusions from what you see. Also it is an organized way of finding objective answers to questions every business owner and manager must answer in order to succeed. Market research focuses and organizes marketing information, ensuring that it is timely and that it provides what you need to:

▲ Reduce business risks

▲ Spot problems and potential problems in your current market

▲ Identify and profit from sales opportunities

▲ Get basic facts about your markets to help you make better decisions and set up plans of action

If viewed from this standpoint, market research is an invaluable tool that can save you time, effort, and money.

Time for a
Pop Quiz

During this activity, you will answer the following questions:

1. Do you have a marketing plan?
Yes____ No____

2. If yes, which elements described in the preceding pages did you NOT include?

3. Have you conducted any marketing research?

4. If yes, how and what methods did you use?

5. If no, why?

THE BUSINESS PLAN
Competition

Competition is a way of life. We compete for jobs, promotions, scholarships to institutions of higher learning, in sports, and in almost every aspect of our lives. Nations compete for the consumer in the global marketplace as do individual business owners. Advances in technology can send the profit margins of a successful business into a tailspin causing them to plummet overnight or within a few hours. When considering these and other factors, we can conclude that business is a highly competitive, volatile arena. Because of this volatility and competitiveness, it is important to know your competitors.

Questions like these can help you:

- Who are your five nearest direct competitors?

- Who are your indirect competitors?

- How are their businesses: Steady? Increasing? Decreasing?

- What have you learned from their operations? From their advertising?

- What are their strengths and weaknesses?

- How does their product or service differ from yours?

Start a file on each of your competitors. Keep manila envelopes of their advertising and promotional materials and their pricing strategy techniques. Review these files periodically, determining when and how often they advertise, sponsor promotions and offer sales. Study the copy used in the advertising and promotional materials. For example, is their copy short? Descriptive? Catchy? How much do they reduce prices for sales? Using this technique can help you to understand your competitors better and how they operate their businesses.

THE BUSINESS PLAN
Pricing and Sales

Your pricing strategy is another marketing technique you can use to improve overall competitiveness. Get a feel for the pricing strategy your competitors are using. That way you can determine if your prices are in line with competitors in your market area along with industry averages.

Some of the pricing strategies are:

- retail cost and pricing

- competitive position

- pricing below competition

- pricing above competition

- price lining

- multiple pricing

- service costs and pricing (for service businesses only)

- service components

- material costs

- labor costs

- overhead costs

Appendix 1 contains a sample entitled Price/Quality Matrix. Review it for ideas on pricing strategies for your competitors. Determine which of the strategies they use, if it is effective, and why.

The key to success is to have a well-planned strategy, to establish your policies and to constantly monitor prices and operating costs to ensure profits. Even in a franchise where the franchisor provides operational procedures and materials, it is a good policy to keep abreast of the changes in the marketplace because these changes can affect competitiveness and profit margins.

THE BUSINESS PLAN
Advertising and Public Relations

Having a good product or service and not advertising and promoting it is like not having a business at all.

How you advertise and promote your goods and services may make or break your business. Having a good product or service and not advertising and promoting it is like not having a business at all. Many business owners operate under the mistaken concept that the business will promote itself and channel money that should be used for advertising and promotions to other areas of the business. Advertising and promotions, however, are the lifeline of a business and need to be treated as such.

Devise a plan that uses advertising and networking as a means to promote your business. Develop a short, descriptive copy (text material) that clearly identifies your goods or services, its location, and price. Use catchy phrases to arouse the interest of your readers, listeners or viewers. In the case of a franchise, the franchisor will provide advertising and promotional materials as part of the franchise package. You may need approval to use any materials that you and your staff develop. Whether or not this is the case, as a courtesy, allow the franchisor the opportunity to review, comment on and, if required, approve these materials before using them. Make sure the advertisements you create are consistent with the image the franchisor is trying to project. Remember the more care and attention you devote to your marketing program, the more successful your business will be.

THE BUSINESS PLAN -
The Management Plan

Managing a business requires more than just the desire to be your own boss. It demands dedication, persistence, the ability to make decisions, and to manage both employees and finances.

Your management plan, along with your marketing and financial management plans, set the foundation for and facilitate the success of your business.

...it is imperative that you know what skills you possess and those you lack since you will have to hire personnel to compensate the weaknesses.

Like plants and equipment, people are resources -- they are the most valuable asset a business has. You will soon discover that employees and staff will play an important role in the total operation of your business. Consequently, it is imperative that you know what skills you possess and those you do not. You will have to hire personnel to supply the skills you lack. Additionally, it is imperative that you know how to manage and treat your employees. Make them a part of the team. Keep them informed of, and get their feedback regarding, changes. Employees oftentimes have excellent ideas that can lead to new market areas, innovations to existing products or services or new product lines or services, which can improve your overall competitiveness.

Your management plan should answer questions such as:

● How does your background/business experience help you in this particular business?

● What are your weaknesses and how can you compensate for them?

● Who will be on the management team?

● What are their strengths/weaknesses?

● What are their duties?

● Are these duties clearly defined?

The franchisor should assist you with managing your franchise... take advantage of their expertise.

- If a franchise, what type of assistance can you expect from the franchisor?

- Will this assistance be ongoing?

- What are your current personnel needs?

- What are your plans for hiring and training personnel?

- What salaries, benefits, vacations, and holidays will you offer? If a franchise, are these issues covered in the management package the franchisor will provide?

- What benefits, if any, can you afford at this point?

If a franchise, the operating procedures, manuals and materials devised by the franchisor should be included in this section of the business plan. Study these documents carefully when writing your business plan, and be sure to incorporate this material. The franchisor should assist you with managing your franchise. Take advantage of their expertise and develop a management plan that will ensure the success for your franchise and satisfy the needs and expectations of employees, as well as the franchisor.

THE BUSINESS PLAN -
The Financial Management Plan

Sound financial management is one of the best ways for your business to remain profitable and solvent. How well you manage the finances of your business is the cornerstone of every successful business venture. Each year thousands of potentially successful businesses fail because of poor financial management. As a business owner, you will need to identify and implement policies that will lead to and ensure that you will meet your financial obligations.

To effectively manage your finances, plan a sound, realistic budget by determining the actual amount of money needed to open your business (start-up costs) and the amount needed to maintain it (operating costs). The first step to building a sound financial plan is to devise a start-up budget. Your start-up budget will usually include such one-time-only costs as major equipment, utility deposits, down payments, etc.

The start-up budget should allow for these expenses.

Start Up Budget

- personnel (costs prior to opening)

- legal/professional fees

- occupancy

- licenses/permits

- equipment

- insurance

- supplies

- advertising/promotions

- salaries/wages

- accounting
- income
- utilities
- payroll expenses

Your operating budget should also include money to cover the first three to six months of operation.

An operating budget is prepared when you are actually ready to open for business. The operating budget will reflect your priorities in terms of how you spend your money, the expenses you will incur and how you will meet those expenses (income). Your operating budget should also include money to cover the first three to six months of operation. Allow for the following expenses.

Operating Budget

- personnel
- insurance
- rent
- depreciation
- loan payments
- advertising/promotions
- legal/accounting
- miscellaneous expenses
- supplies
- payroll expenses
- salaries/wages
- utilities
- dues/subscriptions/fees
- taxes
- repairs/maintenance

The financial section of your business plan should include any loan applications you have filed, a capital equipment and supply list, balance sheet, breakeven analysis, pro-forma income projections (profit and loss statement) and pro-forma cash flow. The income statement and cash flow projections should include a three-year summary, detail by month for the first year, and detail by quarter for the second and third years.

The accounting system and the inventory control system that you will be using is generally addressed in this section of the business plan also. If a franchise, the franchisor may stipulate in the franchise contract the type of accounting and inventory systems you may use. If this is the case, he or she should have a system already intact which you will be required to adopt. Should you develop the accounting and inventory systems yourself, have an outside financial advisor develop the systems or the franchisor provides the systems, you will need to acquire a thorough understanding of each segment and how it operates. Your financial advisor can assist you in developing this section of your business plan.

...accounting and inventory systems...you will need to acquire a thorough understanding of each segment and how it operates.

The following questions should help you determine the amount of start-up capital you will need to purchase and open a franchise.

▶ How much money do you have?

▶ How much money will you need to purchase the franchise?

▶ How much money will you need for start-up?

▶ How much money will you need to maintain your business?

Other questions that you will need to consider are:

▶ What type of accounting system will you use? Is it a single entry or dual entry system?

> ❱ What will be your sales goals and profit goals for the upcoming year? If a franchise, will the franchisor set your sales and profit goal or, will he or she expect you to reach and retain a certain sales level and profit margin?

> ❱ What financial projections will you need to include in your business plan?

> ❱ What kind of inventory control system will you use?

Unless you are thoroughly familiar with financial statements, get help in preparing your cash flow and income statements and your balance sheet.

Your plan should include an explanation of all projections. Unless you are thoroughly familiar with financial statements, get help in preparing your cash flow and income statements and your balance sheet. Your aim is not to become a financial wizard, but to understand the financial tools well enough to reap the benefits. Your accountant or financial advisor can help you accomplish this goal.

Sample balance sheets, income projections (profit and loss statements) and cash flow statements are included in Appendix 2, Financial Management. For a detailed explanation of these and other more complex financial concepts, contact your local SBA office. Look under the U.S. Government section of the local telephone directory or you can find detailed information about the SBA through your Grant Seeker Pro™ CD.

THE BUSINESS PLAN - APPENDIX 1

MARKETING

I. THE MARKETING PLAN

II. PRICE/QUALITY MATRIX

III. MARKETING TIPS, TRICKS & TRAPS

THE ENTREPRENEUR'S

MARKETING PLAN

This is the marketing plan of _____

I. MARKET ANALYSIS

   A. Target Market - Who are the customers?

      1. We will be selling primarily to (check all that apply):

Percent of Business	
Private Sector	%
Wholesalers	
Retailers	
Government	
Other	

THE MARKETING PLAN

2. We will be targeting customers by:

    a. Product line/services.

       We will target specific lines

       _____

    b. Geographic area? Which areas?

       _____

    c. Sales? We will target sales of _____

    d. Industry? Our target industry is

       _____

    e. Other? _____

3. How much will our selected market spend on our type of product or service this coming year?

    $_____

B. Competition

    1. Who are our competitors?

    NAME   _____

    ADDRESS_____

Years in Business   _____

Market Share   _____

Price/Strategy   _____

Product/Service
Features   _____

    NAME_____

    ADDRESS _____

Years in Business   _____

Market Share   _____

Price/Strategy   _____

Product/Service
Features   _____

2. How competitive is the market?

High   _____

Medium   _____

Low   _____

THE MARKETING PLAN

THE MARKETING PLAN

3. List your strengths and weaknesses compared to our competition (consider such areas as location, size of resources, reputation, services, personnel, etc.)

Strengths   Weaknesses

1. _____   1. _____

2. _____   2. _____

3. _____   3. _____

4. _____   4. _____

C. Environment

1. The following are some important economic factors that will affect our product or service (such as trade area growth, industry health, economic trends, taxes, rising energy prices, etc.):

_____

_____

_____

2. The following are some important legal factors that will affect our market:

_____

_____

_____

3. The following are some important governmental factors:

_____

_____

_____

4. The following are other environmental factors that will affect our market, but over which we have no control:

_____

_____

_____

THE MARKETING PLAN

PRICE/QUALITY MATRIX

I. PRODUCT OR SERVICE ANALYSIS

A. Description

1. Describe here what our product/service is and what it does:

_____

_____

_____

B. Comparison

1. What advantages does our product/service have over those of the competition (consider such things as unique features, patents, expertise, special training, etc.)?

_____

_____

_____

2. What disadvantages does it have?

_____

_____

_____

C. Some Considerations

1. Where will we get our materials and supplies?

_____

_____

_____

List other considerations:

_____

_____

_____

II. MARKETING STRATEGIES - MARKET MIX

A. Image

1. First, what kind of image do we want to have (such as cheap but good, or exclusiveness, or customer-oriented or highest quality, or convenience, or speed, or ...)?

_____

B. Features

1. List the features we will emphasize:

a. _____

b. _____

c. _____

C. Pricing

1. We will be using the following pricing strategy:

a. Markup on cost   _____   What % markup? _____

b. Suggested price   _____

c. Competitive   _____

d. Below competition _____

e. Premium price   _____

f. Other   _____

PRICE/QUALITY
MATRIX

2. Are our prices in line with our image?

  YES___   NO___

3. Do our prices cover costs and leave a margin of profit?

  YES___   NO___

D. Customer Services

1. List the customer services we provide:

  a. _____

  b. _____

  c. _____

2. These are our sales/credit terms:

  a. _____

  b. _____

  c. _____

3. The competition offers the following services:

  a. _____

  b. _____

  c. _____

E. Advertising/Promotions

1. These are the things we wish to say about the business:

_____

_____

_____

2. We will use the following advertising/promotion sources:

    a. Television   _____

    b. Radio   _____

    c. Direct mail   _____

    d. Personal contacts   _____

    e. Trade associations   _____

    f. Newspaper   _____

    g. Magazines   _____

    h. Yellow Pages   _____

    i. Billboard   _____

    j. Other   _____

PRICE/QUALITY MATRIX

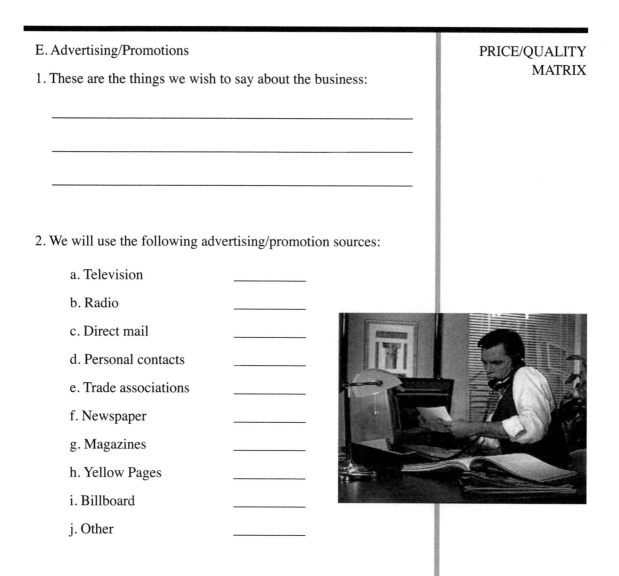

3. The following are the reasons why we consider the media we have chosen to be the most effective:

_____

_____

_____

MARKETING TIPS, TRICKS & TRAPS

I. MARKETING STEPS

A. Classifying Your Customers' Needs

B. Targeting Your Customer(s)

C. Examining Your "Niche"

D. Identifying Your Competitors

E. Assessing and Managing Your Available Resources

   – Financial

   – Human

   – Material

   – Production

NOTES AND STRATEGIES FOR YOUR BUSINESS

II. MARKETING POSITIONING

MARKETING TIPS,
TRICKS & TRAPS

A. Follower versus Leader

B. Quality versus Price

C. Innovator versus Adapter

D. Customer versus Product

E. International versus Domestic

F. Private Sector versus Government

NOTES AND STRATEGIES FOR YOUR BUSINESS

MARKETING TIPS,
TRICKS & TRAPS

III. SALES STRATEGY

A. Use Customer-Oriented Selling Approach -
by Constructing Agreement

1. Phase One: Establish Rapport with Customer -
by agreeing to discuss what the customer
wants to achieve.

2. Phase Two: Determine Customer Objective and
Situational Factors - by agreeing on what
the customer wants to achieve and those
factors in the environment that will influence these results.

3. Phase Three: Recommend a Customer Action Plan -
by agreeing that using your product/
service will indeed achieve what customer
wants.

4. Phase Four: Obtaining Customer Commitment -
by agreeing that the customer will
acquire your product/service.

5. Phase Five: Emphasize Customer Advantage

Must be Read

> When a competitive advantage cannot be demonstrated, it will not translate into a benefit.

Must be Important to the Customer:

> When the perception of competitive advantage varies between supplier and customer, the customer wins.

Must be Specific:

> When a competitive advantage lacks specificity, it translates into mere puffery and is ignored.

Must be Promotable:

> When a competitive advantage is proven, it is essential that your customer know it, lest it not exist at all.

NOTES AND STRATEGIES FOR YOUR BUSINESS

MARKETING TIPS, TRICKS & TRAPS

IV. BENEFITS VS. FEATURES

A. The six "Os" of organizing Customer Buying Behavior

ORIGINS of purchase:	Who buys it?
OBJECTIVES of purchase:	What do they need/buy?
OCCASIONS of purchase:	When do they buy it?
OUTLETS of purchase:	Where do they buy it?
OBJECTIVES of purchase:	Why do they buy it?
OPERATIONS of purchase:	How do they buy it?

B. Convert features to benefits using the "...Which Means..." Transition

C. Sales Maxim: "Unless the proposition appeals to their INTEREST, unless it satisfies their DESIRES, and unless it shows them a GAIN--then they will not buy!"

D. Quality Customer Leads

Level of need	Ability to pay
Authority to pay	Accessibility
Sympathetic attitude	Business history
One-source buyer	Reputation (price or quality

NOTES AND STRATEGIES FOR YOUR BUSINESS

MARKETING TIPS,
TRICKS & TRAPS

MARKETING TIPS,
TRICKS & TRAPS

V. CONVERT FEATURES INTO BENEFITS-- THE "...WHICH MEANS..." TRANSITION

FEATURES   *"which means"*   BENEFITS

FEATURES	BENEFITS
Performance	Time Saved
Reputation	Reduced Cost
Components	Prestige
Colors	Bigger Savings
Sizes	Greater Profits
Exclusive	Greater Convenience
Uses	Uniform Production
Applications	Uniform Accuracy
Ruggedness	Continuous Output
Delivery	Leadership
Service	Increased Sales
Price	Economy of Use
Design	Ease of Use
Availability	Reduced Inventory
Installation	Low Operating Cost
Promotion	Simplicity
Lab Tests	Reduced Upkeep
Terms	Reduced Waste
Workmanship	Long Life

VI. BUYING MOTIVES

RATIONAL	EMOTIONAL
Economy of Purchase	Pride of Appearance
Economy of Use	Pride of Ownership
Efficient Profits	Desire of Prestige
Increased Profits	Desire for Recognition
Durability	Desire to Imitate
Accurate Performance	Desire for Variety
Labor-Saving	Safety
Time-Saving	Fear
Simple Construction	Desire to Create
Simple Operation	Desire for Security
Ease of Repair	Convenience
Ease of Installation	Desire to Be Unique
Space-Saving	Curiosity
Increased Production	
Availability	
Complete Servicing	
Good Workmanship	
Low Maintenance	
Thorough Research	
Desire to be Unique	
Curiosity	

MARKETING TIPS,
TRICKS & TRAPS

VI. PRICE / QUALITY MATRIX
     SALES APPEALS

PRICE/QUALITY

	HIGH	MEDIUM	LOW
HIGH	"Rolls Royce" Strategy	"We Try Harder" Strategy	"Best Buy" Strategy
MEDIUM	"Out Performs" Strategy	"Piece of the Rock" Strategy	"Smart Shopper" Strategy
LOW	"Feature Packed" Strategy	"Keeps on Ticking" Strategy	"Bargain Hunter" Strategy

THE BUSINESS PLAN - APPENDIX 2

INFORMATION RESOURCES

I.   U.S. SMALL BUSINESS ADMINISTRATION (SBA)

The SBA offers an extensive selection of information on most business management topics, from how to start a business to exporting your products.

This information is listed in "Resource Directory for Small Business Management." For a free copy contact your nearest SBA office.

The SBA has offices throughout the country. Consult the U.S. Government section in your telephone directory for the office nearest you. The SBA offers a number of programs and service including training and educational programs, counseling services, financial programs and contract assistance. Ask about

A. Service Corps of Retired Executives (SCORE), a national organization sponsored by SBA of over 13,000 volunteer business executives who provide free counseling, workshops and seminars to prospective and existing small business people.

B. Small Business Development Centers (SBDCs), sponsored by the SBA in partnership with state and local governments, the educational community and the private sector. They provide assistance, counseling and training to prospective and existing business people.

C. Business Information Centers (BICs), offering state-of-the-art technology, informational resources and on-site counseling for start-up and expanding businesses to create business, marketing and other plans, do research, and receive expert training and assistance.

For more information about SBA business development programs and services, call the SBA Small Business Answer Desk at 1-800-U-ASK-SBA (827-5722).

II. Other U.S. Government Resources

Many publications on business management and other related topics are available from the Government Printing Office (GPO). GPO bookstores are located in 24 major cities and listed in the Yellow Pages under the "bookstore" heading. You can request a "Subject Bibliography" by writing to Government Printing Office, Superintendent of Documents, Washington, DC 20402-9328.

Many federal agencies offer publications of interest to small businesses. There is a nominal fee for some, but most are free. What follows is a selected list of government agencies that provide publications and other services targeted to small businesses. To get their publications, contract the regional offices listed in the telephone directory or write to the addresses below:

Consumer Information Center (CIC)
P.O. Box 100
Pueblo, CO 81002

The CIC offers a consumer information catalog of federal publications.

Consumer Product Safety Commission (CPSC)
Publications Request
Washington, DC 20207

The CPSC offers guidelines for product safety requirements.

U.S. Department of Agriculture (USDA)
12th Street and Independence Avenue, SW
Washington, DC 20250

The USDA offers publications on selling to the USDA. Publications and programs on entrepreneurship are also available through county extension offices nationwide.

U.S. Department of Commerce (DOC)
Office of Business Liaison
14th Street and Constitution Avenue, NW
Room 5898C
Washington, DC 20230

DOC's Business Assistance Center provides listings of business opportunities available in the federal government. This service also will refer businesses to different programs and services in the DOC and other federal agencies.

U.S. Department of Health and Human Services (HHS) - Public Health Service
Alcohol, Drug Abuse and Mental Health Administration
5600 Fishers Lane
Rockville, MD 20857

Drug Free Workplace Helpline: 1-800-843-4971. Provides information on Employee Assistance Programs.

Resources

163

Resources

National Institute for Drug Abuse Hotline:
1-800-662-4357.

Provides information on preventing substance abuse in the workplace.

The National Clearinghouse for Alcohol and Drug Information:
1-800-729-6686 toll-free.

Provides pamphlets and resource materials on substance abuse.

U.S. Department of Labor (DOL)
Employment Standards Administration
200 Constitution Avenue, NW
Washington, DC 20210

The DOL offers publications on compliance with labor laws.

U.S. Department of Treasury
Internal Revenue Service (IRS)
P.O. Box 25866
Richmond, VA 23260
1-800-424-3676

The IRS offers information on tax requirements for small businesses.

Environmental Protection Agency Office of Small Business Ombudsman
U.S. Environmental Protection Agency (EPA)
Small Business Ombudsman
Room 3423
401 M Street, S.W.
Washington, D.C. 20460
1-800-368-5888 except in DC and VA
202-260-1211 in DC and VA

The EPA offers more than 100 publications designed to help small businesses understand how they can comply with EPA regulations.

U.S. Food and Drug Administration (FDA)
FDA Center for Food Safety and Applied Nutrition
200 C Street, SW
Washington, DC 20204

The FDA offers information on packaging and labeling requirements for food and food-related products.

Resources

For More Information

A librarian can help you locate the specific information you need in reference books. Most libraries have a variety of directories, indexes and encyclopedias that cover many business topics. They also have other resources, such as

▲ Trade association information

Ask the librarian to show you a directory of trade associations. Associations provide a valuable network of resources to their members through publications and services such as newsletters, conferences and seminars.

▲ Books

Many guidebooks, textbooks and manuals on small business are published annually. To find the names of books not in your local library check Books In Prints, a directory of books currently available from publishers.

▲ Magazine and newspaper articles

Business and professional magazines provide information that is more current than those found in books and textbooks. There are a number of indexes to help you find specific articles in periodicals.

In addition to books and magazines, many libraries offer free workshops, lend skill-building tapes and have catalogues and brochures describing continuing education opportunities.

GRANT SEEKER PRO™

Grant Seeker Pro™
How to Use the Software

 his Section will give you some basic information to get you started using your Grant Seeker Pro™ CD-ROM product. The data on the CD-ROM contains almost 1500 separate programs of the Federal Government, which in turn provides a wide range of assistance to individuals, organizations and governmental entities. This CD is a self-contained product which means that there are no special programs required.

The first screen you will see when you insert the CD is the installation program. Simply follow the on-screen instructions to complete the installation.

Grant Seeker Pro™ Search makes it easier than ever to get instant results to keyword searches. Best of all there is no need for an internet connection! All of the information is contained right on your Grant Seeker Pro™ CD-ROM. You can search for applicable laws and eligibilities. In case of multiple results, the search function will index the result, and maintain that index while you browse.

You can specify several search criteria. For example, you can search for programs by program name, program number, assistance types, categories etc. You can even search for programs on the basis of related programs.

The "File" function on your screen's top tool bar allows you to access application processing wizards, the business plan wizard, catalog modification tools, etc. The "Help" function allows you access to the help files that can guide you through all of the various functions of Grant Seeker Pro™.

Everything required to run the program is contained within the program itself.

In the catalog view, click on the plus sign to expand the sections within, or click on the minus sign to collapse for a more convenient view.

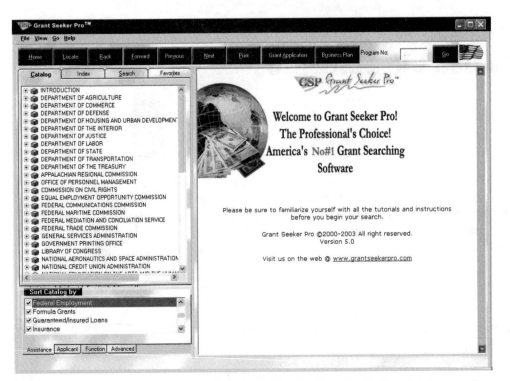

The "Search" tab gives the facility for keyword search. Type in virtually any word you want and it will return results. For example if you type in the word "minority" you will receive 160 responses. If you type in "child care" you receive 28 responses. If you receive too many results, refine your search. Conversely, if you receive too few results, try to broaden your search by using multiple words.

Because The U. S. federal funding programs are so varied in scope and purpose a single application kit for all programs is not available. Once you have made a list of the potential funders, you are ready to use the Grant Application Wizard to create request letters and applications.

To do this, first bring up the program you wish to apply to in the catalog view. Once you have the program listed on the right side, click on Grant Application on the top tool bar. This will then open the Grant Application Wizard which will allow you to create the necessary letter and application. At the bottom of the wizard there is a link that you can use to switch between the Grant Application Instructions and the program that you are applying to. To display the instructions, click on the tab at the top. The directions will also redisplay automatically when you click on either the "Next" or "Back" buttons in the Grant Application Wizard.

To create an excellent business plan you can click on the "Business Plan Wizard" on the main tool bar. This template has been used by over half a million companies seeking funding. It is the accepted standard by which most banks do business and also the same standard accepted by the Small Business Administration. This basic outline can even be viewed on the SBA website at *www.sba.gov*.

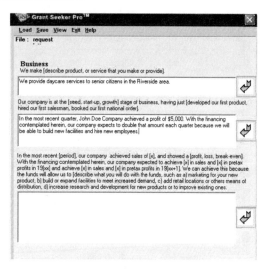

Business Plan Wizard (BPW)

When you open the Business Plan Wizard the first section you will see is a small box giving you a choice to click on "New", "Open" or "Exit." If you click on "New" you will then be asked to save a file onto your hard drive and give it a name. Make sure that you remember where you are saving the file and what you are naming it. Unlike the Grant Application this is not a document that can typically be created within a few minutes. Business plans are fairly extensive and take time and effort to fill out. Once you have named the file and saved it, the first page will automatically welcome you to the Business Plan Wizard. Clicking "Next" will take you to the name and address page where you will fill in some very basic information regarding your company.

The next page begins the process of creating the business plan. Above each empty box is prewritten text that can either be used as an example for your business plan or you can drop into the box and use it exactly as written. Edit in your company name and other pertinent information as needed. To drop in the text, click the arrow beside the box. It is recommended that you save often to ensure retention of information. Always click "Save" before you exit the program so that you can pick up where you left off. Once you have completed a page, click "Save" then "Next" to move to the next section. You can also move back to a preceding page by clicking on the "Back" button.

On the last page of the BPW you will be given the option to view. When you click on "View", your default word processing program will open (WordPad, Notepad, Microsoft Word or other). The completed business plan will then be displayed and you can make any additional editing changes such as font sizes and styles. It is recommended that you do not change this extensively as we have gone to a great deal of trouble to make everything as stylistically correct as possible. You may also save this now as a word file. Make sure that you save your changes in the Business Plan Wizard before you close.

APPLICATION FOR FEDERAL ASSISTANCE

OMB Approval No. 0348-0043

2. DATE SUBMITTED	Applicant Identifier

1. TYPE OF SUBMISSION:

Application
☐ Construction
☐ Non-Construction

Preapplication
☐ Construction
☐ Non-Construction

3. DATE RECEIVED BY STATE	State Application Identifier
4. DATE RECEIVED BY FEDERAL AGENCY	Federal Identifier

5. APPLICANT INFORMATION

Legal Name:

Organizational Unit:

Address (give city, county, State, and zip code):

Name and telephone number of person to be contacted on matters involving this application (give area code)

6. EMPLOYER IDENTIFICATION NUMBER (EIN):

☐☐ - ☐☐☐☐☐☐☐

7. TYPE OF APPLICANT: (enter appropriate letter in box)

A. State	H. Independent School Dist.
B. County	I. State Controlled Institution of Higher Learning
C. Municipal	J. Private University
D. Township	K. Indian Tribe
E. Interstate	L. Individual
F. Intermunicipal	M. Profit Organization
G. Special District	N. Other (Specify) _____

8. TYPE OF APPLICATION:

☐ New	☐ Continuation	☐ Revision

If Revision, enter appropriate letter(s) in box(es) ☐ ☐

A. Increase Award	B. Decrease Award	C. Increase Duration
D. Decrease Duration	Other(specify):

_____

9. NAME OF FEDERAL AGENCY:

10. CATALOG OF FEDERAL DOMESTIC ASSISTANCE NUMBER:

☐☐ - ☐☐☐

TITLE:

11. DESCRIPTIVE TITLE OF APPLICANT'S PROJECT:

12. AREAS AFFECTED BY PROJECT (Cities, Counties, States, etc.):

13. PROPOSED PROJECT		14. CONGRESSIONAL DISTRICTS OF:
Start Date	Ending Date	a. Applicant

b. Project

15. ESTIMATED FUNDING:

		16. IS APPLICATION SUBJECT TO REVIEW BY STATE EXECUTIVE ORDER 12372 PROCESS?
a. Federal	$ .00	
b. Applicant	$ .00	a. YES. THIS PREAPPLICATION/APPLICATION WAS MADE AVAILABLE TO THE STATE EXECUTIVE ORDER 12372 PROCESS FOR REVIEW ON:
c. State	$ .00	
d. Local	$ .00	DATE _____
e. Other	$ .00	b. No. ☐ PROGRAM IS NOT COVERED BY E. O. 12372 ☐ OR PROGRAM HAS NOT BEEN SELECTED BY STATE FOR REVIEW
f. Program Income	$ .00	
g. TOTAL	$ .00	**17. IS THE APPLICANT DELINQUENT ON ANY FEDERAL DEBT?** ☐ Yes If "Yes," attach an explanation. ☐ No

18. TO THE BEST OF MY KNOWLEDGE AND BELIEF, ALL DATA IN THIS APPLICATION/PREAPPLICATION ARE TRUE AND CORRECT, THE DOCUMENT HAS BEEN DULY AUTHORIZED BY THE GOVERNING BODY OF THE APPLICANT AND THE APPLICANT WILL COMPLY WITH THE ATTACHED ASSURANCES IF THE ASSISTANCE IS AWARDED.

a. Type Name of Authorized Representative	b. Title	c. Telephone Number
d. Signature of Authorized Representative		e. Date Signed

Previous Edition Usable
Authorized for Local Reproduction

Standard Form 424 (Rev. 7-97)
Prescribed by OMB Circular A-102

If you get stuck, you can open the "Help" files at any time and view an individual help file that has been created solely for the Business Plan Wizard.

If you need further assistance please write us at techsupport@grantseekerpro.com

Grant Seeker Pro™ will generate forms filled in with the information you provided through the wizard.

INSTRUCTIONS FOR THE SF-424

Public reporting burden for this collection of information is estimated to average 45 minutes per response, including time for reviewing instructions, searching existing data sources, gathering and maintaining the data needed, and completing and reviewing the collection of information. Send comments regarding the burden estimate or any other aspect of this collection of information, including suggestions for reducing this burden, to the Office of Management and Budget, Paperwork Reduction Project (0348-0043), Washington, DC 20503.

PLEASE DO NOT RETURN YOUR COMPLETED FORM TO THE OFFICE OF MANAGEMENT AND BUDGET. SEND IT TO THE ADDRESS PROVIDED BY THE SPONSORING AGENCY.

This is a standard form used by applicants as a required facesheet for preapplications and applications submitted for Federal assistance. It will be used by Federal agencies to obtain applicant certification that States which have established a review and comment procedure in response to Executive Order 12372 and have selected the program to be included in their process, have been given an opportunity to review the applicant's submission.

Item:	Entry:
1.	Self-explanatory.
2.	Date application submitted to Federal agency (or State if applicable) and applicant's control number (if applicable).
3.	State use only (if applicable).
4.	If this application is to continue or revise an existing award, enter present Federal identifier number. If for a new project, leave blank.
5.	Legal name of applicant, name of primary organizational unit which will undertake the assistance activity, complete address of the applicant, and name and telephone number of the person to contact on matters related to this application.
6.	Enter Employer Identification Number (EIN) as assigned by the Internal Revenue Service.
7.	Enter the appropriate letter in the space provided.
8.	Check appropriate box and enter appropriate letter(s) in the space(s) provided:

-- "New" means a new assistance award.

-- "Continuation" means an extension for an additional funding/budget period for a project with a projected completion date.

-- "Revision" means any change in the Federal Government's financial obligation or contingent liability from an existing obligation.

9. Name of Federal agency from which assistance is being requested with this application.

10. Use the Catalog of Federal Domestic Assistance number and title of the program under which assistance is requested.

11. Enter a brief descriptive title of the project. If more than one program is involved, you should append an explanation on a separate sheet. If appropriate (e.g., construction or real property projects), attach a map showing project location. For preapplications, use a separate sheet to provide a summary description of this project.

Item:	Entry:
12.	List only the largest political entities affected (e.g., State, counties, cities).
13.	Self-explanatory.
14.	List the applicant's Congressional District and any District(s) affected by the program or project.
15.	Amount requested or to be contributed during the first funding/budget period by each contributor. Value of in-kind contributions should be included on appropriate lines as applicable. If the action will result in a dollar change to an existing award, indicate *only* the amount of the change. For decreases, enclose the amounts in parentheses. If both basic and supplemental amounts are included, show breakdown on an attached sheet. For multiple program funding, use totals and show breakdown using same categories as item 15.
16.	Applicants should contact the State Single Point of Contact (SPOC) for Federal Executive Order 12372 to determine whether the application is subject to the State intergovernmental review process.
17.	This question applies to the applicant organization, not the person who signs as the authorized representative. Categories of debt include delinquent audit disallowances, loans and taxes.
18.	To be signed by the authorized representative of the applicant. A copy of the governing body's authorization for you to sign this application as official representative must be on file in the applicant's office. (Certain Federal agencies may require that this authorization be submitted as part of the application.)

SF-424 (Rev. 7-97) Back

Word Play

Ahh! The power of words. Whenever writing a grant, word selection is key. Chances are that the individual reading your proposal is a college graduate, probably holding multiple degrees. It would be detrimental for your proposal to read as if written by a child. On the other hand, just because the individual has a degree, you do not need to impress them with your word power either. Using too many big words unnecessarily can hurt you even more. When in doubt, refer to the old adage: K.I.S.S.—*Keep It Simple Silly.*

When writing your proposal you really need to remember to use as many action words as practical (notice we said "practical" not possible). Action words tend to carry more weight than nonaction words. They show a sense of passion for the project.

We strongly recommend that you return to the bookstore where you purchased your Grant Seeker Pro™ and buy a thesaurus. You may also want to have a dictionary on hand. If you are comfortable working on the internet, then two excellent resources for dictionaries and thesauruses are **www.dictionary.com** and **www.m-w.com.**

What follows is a list of action words for your proposals. Refer to them often. When in doubt, look it up!

abandon	advertise	ambitious	aptitude
abundant	advocate	ammunition	artistic
accelerate	affect	amplify	assemble
acceptable	afford to	analyze	assess
accessible	aggressive	animate	assessment
accommodate	aggressively	answer	assimilate
accurate	agree	anxious	associate
acquire	agreement	apply	assume
active	aim	apportion	attack
actively	allocate	appraisal	attainable
adapt	allot	approval	attempt
adventure	alter	approve	authentic

authorization

available

award

aware

basic

basis

bear out

becoming

begin

behalf

behavior

belief

better

blame

blast

blemish

blessed

blessing

block

blunder

bold

bored

bounce-back

boundless

bountiful

bracing

brainy

branch

bridge (as in "Bridge the gap")

brighten

bring

browse

bulldoze

business

busy

calculate

camaraderie

campaign

cancel

candid

canvas

cap

capacity

capitalize

captivating

capture

care

careful

caring

carry

catalyst

catastrophic

catch

catchy

categorical

categorize

causal

caution

cautious

celebrate

certainly

champion (as in "To champion a cause")

chance

change

channel

characteristic

charge

charter

chase

chasm

cheapen

check

chiefly

choice

choose

chronic

chronological

citation

clarity

clash

class

classic

clear-cut

clearly

clever

cliché

closure

cogent

cohesive

cohort

collaborate

collapse

collect

combat

combine	conform	dangerous	depart-from
come-together	confuse	dare	departure
command	congruent	dash	dependable
commend	consequence	dazzle	deplorable
commit	consequently	deal	deposit
commitment	constant	debate	design
compact	continue	decent	desirable
comparative	continuous	decide	desire
compassion	controversy	decision	detail
compel	convert	decisive	detect
complacent	convey	declare	determined
complete	convince	decline	detriment
complex	cooperate	decrease	development
complicate	coordinate	deduct	developmental
component	correct	deep-rooted	dialogue
compress	courageous	defend	differ
compromise	cover	defiant	differences
compulsory	create	deficient	diffuse
concentrate	creative	definite	dignify
concise	credible	delegate	dignity
concur	crucial	deliberate	diligence
conducive	cultivate	deliver	diplomacy
confident	curious	demanding	direct
confirm	cut	demonstrate	direction

disadvantaged

discern

discipline

discordant

discourse

discovery

discrepancy

discretion

discriminate

disengage

disjointed

disparity

display

dissatisfaction

dissension

distinct

distribute

divergent

diverse

diversify

doubtful

draft

drain

dramatic

draw

drive

dubious

duplicate

dwindle

dynamic

eager

earmark

eclectic

educate

educational

effect

effective

efficient

effort

effortless

elaborate

elevate

eliminate

elusive

embrace

empower

enable

encompass

encounter

encouragement

encroach

endeavor

endorsement

endure

engage

enhance

enjoin

enlighten

enormous

enterprise

enthusiastic

entrepreneurial

equality

equipage

equitable

equity

eradicate

erase

err

essential

evaluate

evaluation

event

evidence

exact

exacting

examine

example

exceed

excellent

exceptional

exchange

execute (not to kill but to carry out a plan)

exemplary

exercise

exhaust

exhaustive

exhibit

expect

expectation

experiment

expert

expertise

explain

explicit

expose
express
extend
extensive
extraordinary
extreme
exuberance
facilitate
factor
faddish
fairly
fallacy
familiar
family
feasible
feeling
fertile
fight
finance
find
finite
firm
fitting
flagrant

flexible
flood
flourish
fluctuate
foggy
follow
foolish
force
forceful
forerunner
formerly
fortify
forward
fragmentary
frame
frenzied
frenzy
frequent
frequently
fresh
fruition
frustration
full
full-fledged

full-scale
functional
fund
fundamental
furor
fusion
futile
future
gain
galvanize
gauge

generally
generate
generous
genius
genuine
germane
gimmick
glaring
govern
gradual
grandstand

grant

grave

growth

guarantee

guide

gutsy

halt

handy

haphazard

happen

harbinger

harbor

harmonious

harsh

hazard

healthy

heartfelt

heighten

help

heroic

hesitant

highly

hold

honest

honorable

hottest

however

humane

humor

hustle

hypothesis

ideal

identical

identify

ignite

ignorance

ill-advised

illuminate

illustrate

imagine

immediate

immense

impair

impart

impartiality

impeccable

impediment

implement

important

impressive

imprint

incentive

incompetence

inconsistent

incorporate

increase

increasingly

incur

indicate

individualism

inequality

inequitable

in-essence

inevitable

inexperienced

infinite

influence

information

initiate

injustice

inquire

inquiry

inspire

institute

instruct

in-summary

intellect

intelligent

intensify

interest

interestingly

interpret

intrepid

introduce

invent

investigate

invigorate

involve

isolate

itemize

jargon

jell

join

journal

judge

just

justify	obsolete	overlap	perceptive
juvenile	obstacle	overwhelming	perennial
keen	obvious	ownership	perfection
keep	obviously	package	performance
key	odyssey	painstaking	peripheral
kindle	official	pair	perpetuate
kinetic	offspring	paltry	persist
kinship	open-minded	paradigm	personality
knowledge	operate	paradox	perspective
kudos	opportune	paradoxically	persuasion
label	opportunity	parallel	pertinent
laboratory	opposition	parity	phase-out
lackadaisical	opt	partial	phases
landmark	optimistic	participant	philosophy
lapse	optimum	particularly	plainly
largely	order	passion	play
latitude	ordinary	passionate	plea
mete-out	organize	patient	plentiful
miniscule	original	pattern	plunge
nurture	orthodox	peak	point
object	otherwise	peerless	polarize
objective	outcome	penetrate	polish
obscure	outline	penetration	ponder
observe	overall	perception	pool

popular	primarily	quality	reality
position	primary	quantify	realm
positive	prime	quasi	reason
positively	priority	quest	reasonable
potent	proclivity	question	rebound
potential	produce	quick	recall
poverty	profess	quota	receive
power	profuse	quotation	receptive
powerful	progressive	quote	reciprocal
practical	project	race	reciprocate
practicality	promote	raise	recognize
practice	proof	ramification	recommend
pragmatic	proponent	rampant	record
praise	propose	rank	recovery
precedence	protect	rapid	rectify
precise	protract	rare	reduce
precursor	provide	rarely	reduction
preferable	prudence	reach	refer
prerequisite	prudent	reachable	refine
pressure	public	react	reflect
prestigious	pull	reaction	reflective
presumption	purchase	readiness	reflex
prevail	purposeful	realism	reform
priceless	qualify	realistically	refreshing

regarding	respectable	scholarship	simplistic
regenerate	responsive	scientific	simulate
register	restore	score	simulation
regress	restriction	scrutinize	sincere
regulate	revamp	search	society
reinforce	reveal	seek	solid
relate	reverse	seize	special
relieve	revisit	select	specify
remarkable	revolutionary	self-starting	speculate
remedial	reward	sensible	sponsor
remodel	rewarding	sensitive	sponsorship
render	rhetorical	separate	spread
renovate	right	sequence	spur
repair	rightly	sequential	squelch
repeat	rigor	serious	standards
report	robust	setting	step-by-step
represent	sample	sham	stimulate
require	satisfactory	sharpen	stipulation
rescue	savor	shift	strategic
research	scale	shock	strengthen
resilient	scam	shortly	strike
resist	scan	sidetrack	struggle
resolve	scant	significant	study
resourceful	scarcity	simple	subject

subtle

successful

suggest

summarize

superior

supplementary

supportive

surely

survey

sustain

synthesis

systemize

tact

take

talk

tap

teaching

team-player

teamwork

tedious

temporary

tendency

tenure

term

terminate

territory

theory

therapeutic

therefore

think

thorough

thoughtful

threatening

tighten

tireless

together

tolerate

track

traditionally

transfer

translate

treasure

tremendous

trend

trim

trivial

true

trust

try

turn

typically

unavoidable

unbridled

uncertain

unclear

uncommon

unconditional

unconventional

undeniable

undercurrent

understand

understanding

undertake

undo

uneven

unique

unit

unite

unorthodox

unprecedented

unsatisfactory

uplift

uproar

urge

use

useful

utilize

valid

validate

valuable

values

vantage

variable

variation

varying

vent

venture

veracity

verify

vibrant

view

viewpoint

vigilant

vigorous

violate

virtually

vision	warrant	widen	zap
vital	waste	widespread	zeal
vitality	watchdog	wisdom	zealous
vivid	watertight	withstand	zest
vocal	way	work	zone
void	weaken	workable	zoom
volatile	weave	write	zoom
voracious	wedge	wrong	zoom
vulnerable	weighty	yardstick	zoom
wager	welcome	yearly	zoom
wake	well-balanced	yield	zoo
waken	wellness		
wanting	wholeness		
warn	wholly